To Julia,

A good friend
for always.

All the best —

Love,

Mary Claire
2007

OSAKA HEAT

A NOVEL

Mary Claire Mahaney

Bloomington, IN

authorHOUSE®

Milton Keynes, UK

AuthorHouse™
1663 Liberty Drive, Suite 200
Bloomington, IN 47403
www.authorhouse.com
Phone: 1-800-839-8640

AuthorHouse™ UK Ltd.
500 Avebury Boulevard
Central Milton Keynes, MK9 2BE
www.authorhouse.co.uk
Phone: 08001974150

This book is a work of fiction. People, places, events, and situations are the product of the author's imagination. Any resemblance to actual persons, living or dead, or historical events, is purely coincidental.

First published by AuthorHouse 5/17/2007

ISBN: 978-1-4259-9082-4 (sc)

Library of Congress Control Number: 2007900233

Printed in the United States of America
Bloomington, Indiana

This book is printed on acid-free paper.

For Herb, who feeds me

The strongest principle of growth lies in human choice.

—George Eliot

... and the truth shall set you free.

—Mark 8:32

Tokyo-bound
Monday, July 3, 2000

His bulk trapping me in the window seat, the plump German—Mr. Berg, the flight attendant called him—adjusted his seat backward, jammed the coin-sized pillow between his substantial shoulder and his head, and nodded off to sleep. We were somewhere over Canada. Herr Berg snored, his thighs splayed outward from his hips, his knees lodged against the seatback in front of him. I rang for a glass of water to take another sleeping pill and found my bookmarked page in *The End of the Affair*.

I couldn't read, though, and because of my menu fiasco, my appetite was nowhere near sated. I'd planned on miso soup, seaweed salad, and lots of sushi—I had my travel agent specify Japanese meals—yet that godforsaken chicken cordon bleu was my bill of fare. No Japanese meals today, or at least any they were willing to serve me. I can't believe I upgraded to business class for this.

My new journal's so fresh. It has a nice smell, the crispness of something like Pinot Grigio rising from its pages. It was an impulse purchase, but I'm glad I bought it. In christening this little book, I can't write fast enough about what has happened already. Still, I abhor making these first indelible marks. I'm apprehensive, but why? I'm simply writing.

Which leads me to say for the record, I'm not *journaling*. I hate to hear, to see, to smell, to touch, or to taste nouns used as verbs or verbs used as nouns. If the principal at dear old Confederate High—highest SAT scores in the state, mind you—uses *walk the walk* once more, I'll rub his nose in Traveller's hindquarters. That darn mascot, Robert E. Lee's horse. I didn't realize I was entering the Civil War South when I moved to Virginia. One would think in all the years I've lived in the Old Dominion I'd be used to the place. There's just no state like the Keystone, the best in the Union.

I wish I were a graceful flyer. I wish I were asleep. Between the pills and the scotches, I'm relaxed, nothing more. I should have conked out long ago. I took a sedative as I got out of the cab at Dulles and another as I waited at the gate, and I swallowed the first of my new little Ambien tablets an hour ago, just as that studly, probably gay, definitely cute, steward cleared my tray table. I suppose I should refer to him as a flight attendant, but all cabin staff should be *stewards*, the way all actors should be *actors*, not half of them *actresses*. At least we don't use *poetess* and *authoress* anymore—those terms sound inane now.

But back to where I started—so far I'm wide awake, my trip to the restroom a scene out of *The Marriage of Figaro* or, more likely, *Monty Python's Flying Circus*. An *excuse me* to *der Berg* didn't stir him, so I started my climb over his massive thighs—the *Massif Central*—to exit our row. Just as I was astraddle him, we hit an air pocket and I was up and down face first on top of the poor man. He woke with a groan as I landed in his lap. Herr Berg, so startled was he, he grabbed me and held me to his chest, his mouth on my neck, my glasses hitting him on the cheek and smudging with the day's grease from his face. I said, "Pardon me, I want to go to the lavatory," but his embrace was strong, the cabin quiet and deserted by the awake. Truth be told—I'm embarrassed to think it, much less to write it down where someone might see—it felt *good*, I enjoy being held by a man. It's been so long. As his hands reached lower, I wondered what would happen next, but he opened his eyes and recovered his senses, and with a voice filled with regret (regret for what?) apologized. *Entschuldigen Sie! Entschuldigen Sie!* he said. I replied, "That's okay. It's quite all right," which made me sound as if I were a tart who often lies on men's laps, and I staggered back to the restroom (past the groggy creep in 5A patting an empty seat and saying, "Come sit here by me, honey") where I looked in the mirror and found my face flushed. Was the flush from the scotch? Or from something else?

I find now that Herr Berg has moved three rows back, leaving me with two seats to myself. I've tried to get comfortable, but I can't move the arm rest—it has those moronic controls in it—so I'm not able to stretch out across the two seats, and my own seat won't lie (not *lay*) flat. My Ambien must be past its shelf date. I'm awake, alert, and able to help the pilots fly. I'll ask for a deck of cards and play solitaire along the Great Circle Route.

And this diary, this labor of love—for whom am I keeping it? For myself? Yes, except someone as private as I am can still fantasize about a readership, even if it's only one other person. Am I keeping it for my dead husband? That's silly. For my parents? Silly too, dead too. For my daughter, Bernie? Not for her immediate enjoyment, not at this rate. That leaves Reggie. For Reggie, then, for my sister. And even though I have a lifetime of sharing secrets with my sister, I'm going to try to forget, as I go along, for whom I'm writing or indeed that I'm writing for anyone but myself. Yes, that's it—I'm going to record what happens on this trip, as documentation for my report (extracted and edited) and for posterity. My grandchildren, may God bless me with them, might find it interesting: *Ginger O'Neill Goes Oriental*. But I go under such stress! I feel like Indiana Jones, on a quest for the Holy Grail. No wonder I can't sleep.

We've lost the day, jetting forward, cheated of time. At least going to Europe you get some semblance of nighttime, flying right into it. Our shades have been lowered, but I'm not fooled. I know it's still daylight. In fact it's almost tomorrow. I expect a nasty case of jet lag at this rate. Or as I hear the Japanese say, *jet rag*. I'm going to be one.

Tokyo, Day Nice Hotel
Tuesday, July 4

I know it's rainy season, but nobody told me this is monsoon country. The merchants in the Tokyo evening streets were squeegeeing water out the doors of their shops while Emiko—my short-term tour guide—escorted me along the sidewalk to my hotel. She'd met me at the airport inside customs, after I'd smiled at the customs agent, my most endearing smile, to ease my way. He wasn't having any social intercourse with travelers and asked peremptorily what my business in Japan is. He didn't understand at first; he wasn't exactly expecting me. He seemed concerned when I mentioned the school *exchange*, and called to another agent, whose English was even better than his. Perhaps they thought I was a pedlar, like Moore's Saint Nicholas, hauling a sackful of toys that needed to clear customs. Ultimately I gained entrance by showing them the article from the *Washington Post*, glad that something I packed at the last minute served a purpose.

I tower over Emiko even though I'm not particularly tall—or wide—by American standards. (My Caucasian build takes up way too much space here.) Emiko will deliver me to my train tomorrow morning. I'll be on the *shinkansen*—the bullet train—from Tokyo to Osaka. I could have flown into Osaka but wanted a glimpse of Mount Fuji, mostly so I could say I've seen it. And I wanted to spend a night in Tokyo so I could say I've been here. It was hard enough for me to leave Bernie for my school assignment; I couldn't fathom adding any more time for sightseeing. Maybe she and I can come back together some day. Anyway, I must move on to Osaka in the morning. I'm expected at the school on Thursday.

Emiko was to help me ship my trunk—that monstrosity of a suitcase I packed for my three weeks here—to my host family in Osaka, straight from Narita Airport. But after fifteen minutes of watching bags and then no bags bang around on the carrousel, I filed a claim with the airline. That was a pain in the neck. It took an hour of paperwork and, even though I was assured my bag will be delivered to the Murakamis' house tomorrow, I'm wondering if I'll ever see it again.

With me I've got my handbag and the roller bag I carried onto the plane. The roller bag, in which I have a change of clothes, my toiletries and makeup, and a few other odds and ends, is heavy enough that it's uncomfortable for me to lift it over curbs. The problem is I put too many books in it. I've got the literary works I wanted near me en route, and then my tour books too—I should have cannibalized them, ripping out the pages for areas I'll be visiting and bringing only those pages with me. Any reasonable person would have done that, but I'm a sucker for books, couldn't hurt a friend, at least not a paper friend. I've got an *Insight Guide to Japan*, also a *Tokyo City Guide* (why did I bring it when I was going to be in Tokyo for just one night? maybe I can present it to my hosts as a gift?) and *The Book of Sushi*, forward by Jean-Pierre Rampal. The *Insight Guide* has stunning pictures of Japan—parallel rows of growing crops converging in the middle distance; views of Mount Fuji and views from Mount Fuji; sumo wrestlers knocking each other around in their G-strings; art, architecture, maps. As for the sushi book, well, I could eat my way through this country, and I hope to. I expect Japan to be paradise for a hardcore sushi lover like me.

Emiko rode with me on the bus from the airport while skies flashed and trees thrashed in what I feared was a typhoon—*my disaffected daughter will be an orphan*, I thought, and *serves her right*. When we got off the airport bus at the subway station, Emiko said we could take a cab to the hotel from there, or we could take the subway. It was my choice, she said. I opted for the cab, my feet killing me in my new sandals. (And to think I bought them specifically to walk in! They're supposed to be extra-comfortable, yet my toes were bleeding—they still are—from the rubbing the straps did across my instep.) The cab line wasn't moving, though, for it was the tail end of rush hour and the cabs couldn't get through the watery streets, so after standing in line for fifty minutes we gave up and walked (rather *Emiko* walked, *I* limped) to the subway trains. With each step it felt like the tops of my feet were being hashed or lashed, definitely gashed. It was excruciating. The station and trains were packed and

I didn't even try to find the Band-Aids in my bag. When we finally came out on the street, it was dark but for the electric lights, and I asked Emiko where my hotel was. She pointed straight ahead. I couldn't tell if it was two blocks or ten from where we stood, amidst the squeegeeing, the high rises, and the neon signs.

The stationery says *Day Nice Hotel*. Weird syntax. Are the nights not so nice? I stumbled into the shower stall of a bathroom and hit my calf on the toilet seat. My leg is going black and blue. The threshold to the bathroom is two inches high. It's like being on a ship. My room looks down on the canals. I'm tired and I'm hungry but more tired than hungry, which is fortunate because the hotel kitchen is closed.

I wish my cell phone worked abroad. I didn't even bring it. I ate the dark chocolate I'd stashed in my roller bag and made a trip to the lobby to try to get hold of Bernie and Reggie. The plastic phones are different colors depending on where you're calling—domestic or overseas. There were people in line for the gray phone, and I remembered I'd wanted to buy a phone card before coming to the hotel. The tall young clerk who checked me in came over to help, yet we couldn't communicate, at least not about the phone. He took a slip of paper from his breast pocket and jotted a number on it. "Please call me if I can help you with anything tonight," he wrote. Back here in my room I looked in the mirror and found I had a major smear of chocolate across my mouth. Come to think of it, the clerk was licking his lips.

I don't know what I was thinking about, trying to call home and check up on things—Bernie and Reggie are probably at the pool or already at the Independence Day cookout. I just need to have faith that Bernie is safe. My first night here and I'm in a panic about how things are at home. Do other parents freak out when they leave their kids behind? What am I so afraid of? I thought Bernie would be away at summer camp, as usual, at that nice religious camp in West Virginia, while I went on this first-ever away-from-home business trip, but she managed to flunk chemistry and is spending the summer at Confederate—just my luck! On top of that, she's thrilled to attend a public school for a change. What trouble will she find to get into? Reggie was a doll about agreeing to take care of her, but Reggie's never had a child of her own and does have somewhat loose morals (my apologies, Reg!). My sister isn't stupid—how can a successful tax lawyer be stupid?—but she's not exactly intent on leading a principled life. On the other hand, she and Bernie are crazy about each other. Sometimes I think Bernie likes Reggie more than she likes me. I wish I could speak with Bernie now. She was in a tiff at the airport, and I feel bad about it.

Emiko assured me I'll have no trouble finding my stop in Osaka tomorrow. The trains are punctual, I can just watch my watch, she said. The electronic information board on the train will tell in *romaji*—Emiko said that's what the Japanese call the English alphabet, and I wrote the word down—which station comes next. People who don't know Japanese make the trip all the time, she said. Emiko also reminded me that Japanese people have studied English in school. I sure couldn't tell it when I tried to use the hotel phone.

For my first night in Asia I'm having another sleeping pill, just to get me back on schedule.

Osaka-bound,
Wednesday, July 5

It was a long night, it was a short night, it was a Dickensian night. It was a night overloaded with characters in my flash-by dreams. Correct that: they weren't dreams, only ruminations, for again the Ambien didn't work. I saw Esther Summerson and John Jarndyce, the same scene playing again and again; the two of them, innocent beloved and hopeful lover, standing in Mr. Jarndyce's Growlery, Esther's sweet, perplexed face distorted, as if in a fish bowl, John's mien placid yet intent. The world is Esther's oyster, the pearl of her life gleaming before her, yet she struggles tremendously with her background, her limitations, her sphere.

I am disoriented. I know as I write the word *disorient*, though, that *dis* means *deprived of*, so it's not the right word, not the truth. I'm not deprived of the Orient. I'm deprived of sleep. I've found my Excedrin and will get a can of Coke from the soft drink girl and *I hope* purge myself of this nagging headache. Not *hopefully*, that overused and incorrectly handled adverb. Or *is* it *hopefully* because, after all, I'm full of hope to get rid of the headache? I've no idea—my mind is out of service. At least today I'm wearing my contacts, so maybe I won't look too nerdy when I meet my host family. It's unfortunate that the contacts have accentuated the puffiness of my eyelids. I look as though I spent the night crying.

During the night I thought of Steve, of Bernie, of Reggie, of myself. I tried to look at things objectively but could only conclude, as usual, that there's no objective reality. How could there be? Each of us sees the world from his or her (not *their*, although my word processor would prompt me to choose that pronoun) own perspective. Nonetheless, when I should have been sleeping last night, what I kept coming back to was this: how did I come to be *me*—a forty-one-year-old widow with a beautiful if tempestuous daughter, a generous sister, and discouragingly little prospect of a romantic future? One could say *little* and *discouragingly* are hardly objective, yet they are what I think of as describing my love life. One could also say it's all my own doing and that if I weren't such a stickler for rules I'd be sailing off into the sunset with Mr. Right.

The hotel breakfast was a traditional Japanese morning meal—miso soup, smoked fish, raw eggs, seaweed, rice, sour pickles, natto. The raw eggs were the best part. I flung them over my bowl of warm rice and laid the limp seaweed on top. As for the natto, I couldn't get my mouth around the smell of fermenting soybeans; it was the only thing I left. I was proud of my expertise with chopsticks and hoped the natives noticed. Pride, I'm happy to report, is only a venial sin.

At nine o'clock, Emiko—who asked me if my contacts were bothering me and reflected out loud that many of her clients look as though they've just lost a month's sleep—

put me on this train bound for Osaka. I'm due into the main station, Shinosaka, at noon. It's half past ten and I've quit looking out the window. Mt. Fuji was in a cloud. I'm going back to Graham Greene. Every time I read him I find something new. Greene was such a good writer, and a *Catholic* they always say, as if that makes him a better role model or a deeper thinker or a better person. As if one should overlook Greene's infidelities.

Maurice Bendrix—what a wonderful name Greene came up with for a protagonist—does he bend, is he malleable? The astute reader (me?) knows there must be some transfiguration, some change in store for him, if he's a protagonist in a novel. Bendrix says his parents named him for a literary figure. How romantic to be named for a literary figure, like Edna for the heroine of *The Awakening*, or Tess Durbeyfield. My students never seem to care about these details. Maybe when they're old these things will impress them, if anyone is still reading good books. By that time there may be no delicacy left in literature. Characters, if there are books, may be the likes of Adam Uno and Juliet Romanza.

I wonder what Greene was thinking when he named Bendrix. Did Bendrix's fictitious parents name him for Maurice Maeterlinck, the Belgian author of *Pelléas et Mélisande*, that low-keyed, high-strung drama in which the jealous husband stabs his pregnant wife and her lover to death? Or how about for Maurice Baring? There is that correlation between Greene's dedication of *Affair*

("To C") and the title of Baring's story, *C*. Indeed, Baring was a Catholic friend of Chesterton and Belloc. He could have influenced Greene. (But Catherine was the name of Greene's mistress, so the connection is probably unintentional.) And then there's the protagonist of E. M. Forster's posthumously published book, *Maurice*, which Greene might have seen in manuscript.

No matter for whom he was named, Maurice Bendrix—he'd make a good tenor role in an opera—will be lying again in his narrative. And I don't mean *reclining*. I mean *prevaricating*. Maurice is unreliable, and, as in *The Remains of the Day*, the unreliable narrator is the best thing about the book.

The screaming baby a few rows back is mildly annoying. People are giving the parents dirty looks. (How do I know the parents aren't actually kidnappers?) I'll concentrate on reading.

Suburban Osaka,
Later Wednesday

Namba was a nightmare, in spite of our elaborate pre-trip plans. Aside: this is one occasion when the prefix makes sense. Here and in *pre*destination (which I don't believe in—our wills would serve no purpose if our future were preordained). *Pre* is most of the time used stupidly. Prepackaged—why not packaged or packed? Pre-sliced—what's wrong with sliced? Precooked—give me a break. And my personal bugaboo: preschool. Bernie's nursery school was referred to as Nether Gorge Preschool, at least that was the name on the school's letterhead and the name on the lips of parents delighted to have a child there and the name embroidered over the heart on the teachers' matching polo shirts—different colored shirts for different days of the week—and the name on the bumper stickers the school sold for five dollars each. I refused to buy one. I couldn't see ruining a perfectly good word like *school* with that prefix. (Or a perfectly good bumper with that sticker.) What does *preschool* mean, anyway? Bernie was *in* school, not standing out in front of it. I always made her tuition checks payable to Nether Gorge Nursery School, and they were always cashed. (Now that I've carried on about the prefix, I realize it does not belong before "trip plans" anyway. Plans, by definition, come before the event; here, the trip.)

As I was saying before I ground that dull axe, Namba was a mess. Last month Hiro e-mailed me to say we'd meet at Shinosaka, which according to my Kansai map is smack in the middle of the city. Collecting me in the center of Osaka hardly sounded good for someone who lives in the suburbs, so I wrote back that if he would tell me how to get to the station nearest his house, I'd meet him there. I wanted to try to get all the way from Tokyo to his house on my own. It would have been a real accomplishment. Hiro wrote that we'd compromise—he'd meet me at Namba, which he described as a major hub not far from his house, and then we'd take another train, together, to his neighborhood. He said I should get off the bullet train at Shinosaka and take the stairs to the platform for the local trains. He told me exactly which flight of stairs to take and which side of the platform the Namba-bound train would be on. I'd looked at my printout of his directions as the train rushed into Shinosaka, but when I got off I couldn't recall what the e-mail said. I thought I could figure it out without having to stop and pull out the directions, so I forged ahead. After all, didn't Hiro say my train would be on the *left* as I came up the stairs? (I was distracted by the lunch vendors but held back from complicating things by trying to buy a meal.) Should I have taken that other set of stairs? The sign on the train I boarded said SENRI-CHUO (documenting again; my pocket pad's going to fill up fast too), and I figured Senri-chuo was the station at the end of the line, beyond

Namba; the trains in D.C. display the name of their final station. Hiro said my train would head underground after the first stop. When it didn't go underground, and we were about to pull into the next station, I thought I'd better ask.

"*Sumimasen*," I said to a man across the aisle, glad I knew certain words. "Pardon me" and my sushi vocabulary won't get me far, but they're better than nothing. "Is this the Namba train?" I asked him, hoping the man understood English. He was shuffling papers in his briefcase.

He barely looked up. "No Namba on this train." He returned to his briefcase. I searched the faces of other people in the car. They were in their own capsules, no one making eye contact with me.

"*Sumimasen*," I said again. "I'm looking for Namba." Well, maybe he speaks French. *"Je cherche Namba,"* I tried. Or German. *"Ich will doch Namba!"*

He looked hurt. "No Namba."

Maybe I messed up the German; I've never been good with the grammar. Or the idioms. Let's say I've never been good with German, but I like those capital letters and strings of consonant-rich syllables. Anyway, how could there be no Namba? That's where Hiro told me to go. I yanked my directions out and checked them. I was right: Hiro *did* say to go to Namba. What did this man mean? Or was he being uncooperative on purpose? Maybe the Japanese are like the French.

Namba, Namba. I found myself saying the word out loud. Where had I heard it in the last few hours? If I could just focus my mind. And then, all of a sudden, it came to me—that lip-licking hotel clerk—the one who checked me in at the Day Nice—had said, "Here is the key to your room, Miss, numba seven-zero-four." I loved hearing him say *Miss.*

"I want to *go* to Namba."

Mr. Briefcase didn't smile, he didn't frown, he didn't look up from his papers. "You are on wrong train." I think he said *wrong.* Maybe he said *long.*

When the doors opened I grabbed my roller bag and got off. The platform sign said RYOKUCHIKOEN. A crowd waited for a train going the other direction. I looked for a Westerner. Finding none, I approached a group of women in kimonos.

"Excuse me, do you speak English?" I tried to make eye contact with each of the women but succeeded in speaking only to the air around me.

"I do," said one, finally, in a voice so low the platform noise nearly drowned her out. She had on heavy blue eye shadow, which picked up the blue background in her kimono's fabric. Her makeup reminded me of my high school days and how my friends and I applied our makeup in the school bathroom each morning—heavy foundation, thick mascara, bright blue eye shadow. There was nothing subtle about us parochial school girls.

"I'm trying to find the train to Namba."

"Namba? You want Namba?" She looked at her watch. "We are going to Namba. Come with us."

On the train I clung to her. "I just came from Tokyo," I said.

"What did you do in Tokyo?" The other women were busy talking to each other.

"I'm on a mission."

"Eh?"

So I told her about the competition for coming to Japan, about how my school wants a sister school for student exchanges, faculty exchanges, even administrators' exchanges. (I hope Walk the Walk gets a principal exchange for five years.) I told her how I wasn't going to apply because I don't know Japanese, but that my friend Helen, Confederate's head librarian, cajoled me into filling out the application. I did it just to get Helen off my back (every time she saw me in the hall she said, "You love sushi, don't you, Ginger?"), and I was more surprised than anyone to find myself in the final round of applicants. I didn't relate to the woman all the dishy details, or that beating out the likes of Jim-Bob and Song-mi was quite a coup. Jim-Bob, history teacher *extraordinaire*—just ask him—seemed to have everything the committee wanted—even speaks a little Japanese—but then it came to light he'd been carrying on with Mrs. Walk for years. It seems Madam wanted a baby and Walk couldn't give her one, so she was having Jim-Bob serve her. The man was history himself once the truth was unearthed. Mrs.

Walk, feeling the consequence of each month's passage, *she* was the one who let the word out—she didn't want Jim-Bob gone during one of her fertile moments. And Jim-Bob taught honors history, with those smart kids he adored! Stupid man!

Then I was sure Song-mi was going to win because she's Korean, although I know there's bad blood between Koreans and Japanese. But Song-mi speaks and reads Japanese, and she is brilliant, with her Princeton degree in physics and her education degree at night in record time. The problem with Song-mi, of course, is she smokes cigarettes, but cigarettes are enough to get you in trouble these days, even in tobacco country. One day in her free period Song-mi was seen sneaking off school property, into the woods, for a few puffs. Although what she did wasn't illegal, it *looked* bad. It cost her the appointment. (Helen swears it wasn't she who turned Song-mi in. I'm not so sure.)

I told the woman in the blue kimono that, surprisingly, I ended up with the job. What I didn't say was that it *wasn't* because of my academic background, either my master's in literature, with that yummy emphasis on British and American nineteenth- and twentieth-century fiction, or on account of my Teacher of the Year award six years ago, for at my school all the staff are overeducated and overhonored. Nor did I tell her I *was* chosen because of my personality or that the selection committee wanted me to come to Japan on the school's behalf because I always do the right thing. That I'm a woman (a strike against me in Japan) and that I don't know the language (another strike) aren't important compared to how I comport myself, the committee said. They said they could count on me because my behavior is always exemplary, and that's important when you're an ambassador. What they don't know is that I think about saying a whole lot more than I do say, and who knows when I might decide to blurt it all out? I don't think I'd really do that, but I'd be lying if I didn't acknowledge my fantasies of doing exactly what I want to do.

The committee thought I'd be flattered but it's unsettling. I hate to think I have to do everything right. I have bad moments just like everyone else, although I must agree I'm better behaved than most people I know. As the single mother of a teenager, wanting to set a good example, not wanting to scandalize my daughter (assuming it's possible these days to scandalize a teenager), I try to behave myself.

"You are meeting a teacher from this Osaka private school in Namba?" my train companion asked me.

"One of the teachers and his wife and daughter will be my host family for three weeks. I'll be meeting with teachers, students, administrators, and parents. Their own committee will decide if they want the exchange program. My school's already sure it wants it." I told the woman about how the entire school district is counting on Confederate to win this exchange and about how Confederate doesn't yet offer Japanese as a foreign language but that the district has promised, if we get the exchange, we'll become a Japanese magnet school. I also told her how the district hopes to get a lot of publicity from this venture in the years to come.

I didn't tell her how the district hopes the program will open the door to funding from Japanese companies, but I did mention my visit last month to the home of the Japanese ambassador to the United States. His Washington house is gorgeous, sitting low and Frank Lloyd Wright-like there off Embassy Row, its rectilinear spaces straight from the feudal age. At least that's what I imagined when I visited—mysterious courtiers slinking around in those rooms, sharpened swords hidden in their full, silk trousers. I told the kimono woman how I met the ambassador and his wife and how kind they were to me and how supportive they are of a sister-school program and how they wanted to hear all about Bernie.

"And now I'll be late and will make a bad first impression with my hosts."

"Not so late," she told me. "If you came from Shinosaka, you'll be only thirty minutes late."

I gave her one of my cards and asked her to e-mail me if she'd like. I didn't ask her name. I thought it was too personal a question for a stranger on a train, but I wanted her to know how much I appreciated and trusted her. She thanked me but didn't commit to write. She and her friends disappeared in a scurrying clump after we pulled into Namba.

I wish the *Post* weren't following the story. That picture they ran with the article wasn't very flattering—my hair looked like I'd just tried a new styling gel, which I had. This whole exchange thing is mine to screw up. I'll be in disgrace if I don't win this school. And that snippy little reporter showing up for the send-off at the airport (who invited her, anyway?), making notes while Bernie was behaving like an idiot. I'm sure the reporter noticed too that I boarded when business class was called. I can tell she doesn't like me because I live comfortably. How can I help it if my husband left me comfortable? Money is something people always want to ding you for. They hate you if you have it, hate you if you don't. And she had the bravado to ask me why I teach. "What do you think I would do all day? Shop?" Unfortunately, she printed my response. Helen pointed out she might have been asking why I teach, rather than, say, write.

Hiro had mentioned in his directions that there are at least four Namba stations. He instructed me to exit the subway at the Namba station where my train stopped and to walk underground five minutes to a different Namba station. Why do they have two stations by the same name, much less four? Anyway, I was to meet him and the private train line at Namba Number Two (my words, not his). As it turned out, because I was late, Hiro thought I'd stayed at the first Namba station, so he walked there looking for me, had me paged, called his house, he even called Emiko in Tokyo—I'd given him her phone number just in case. He did everything shy of calling me in Nether Gorge. Meanwhile, I'd gotten off at the correct place and walked five minutes underground, just as Hiro had said to do, to the second Namba station, where he was supposed to be waiting for me. I looked for any man who might be Hiro. He hadn't sent a picture or any description, so I thought he'd be holding a sign saying *Ginger O'Neill*, the way limo drivers do. We must have passed each other underground. I eventually found an English-speaking police officer. He looked like a member of a paramilitary force—brimmed hat, white gloves, striping on his sleeves. He suggested that perhaps Hiro had walked to the first Namba station to try to find me, so the officer phoned over there and had Hiro paged. Sure enough, Hiro answered the page.

They're calling me for dinner. Just one more thing, which I hope doesn't set the tone for my stay: when Hiro and I met and I introduced myself, shaking hands with him, he said, "You should have let me meet you at Shinosaka."

ONE

Tempura

An observer looking down from high above Earth beholds jet trails of Hermes, wraiths of white, ghosts of eternity. Beneath that wispy covering lies the archipelago we fly to, and just off our island chain's coast sits an angry realm of earthquakes and volcanic activity. This blistering zone encircles the Pacific Basin and is known as the Ring of Fire.

Lured from the darkness of her cave by the brilliance of her own reflection, the sun goddess Amaterasu, carrier of dawn, presents to us a world forever turning toward the sun. This land of the rising sun is first among nations free of night's grip. Nihon. Nippon. Japan.

Under the sun, under the moon, the mouth of a great dragon has heaved forth the Kuril Islands, disputed territory, foggy and fishy. In the north, Oyakoba, also known as Atlasov Island (its Russian name), rises from the sea like areole and nipple of a nursing mother's breast. Looking south, our eyes skim over the Hokkaido head, cross the Sapporo-to-Hakodate neck, and run down the Tsugaru Strait, a body of water that hides a tunnel. Our sight settles on the Honshu torso, and we find the dragon's chest swelling alongside the marble-rocked Rikuchu Coast. The upper body of Honshu—Japan's main island—is hollowed out beneath the creature's heart, at Sendai. That same Sendai, home to the Japanese sailing vessel, *Saint John the Baptist*—first Japanese ship to cross the Pacific, its emissaries on a mission to Europe to meet Pope Paul V—had fallen victim by the time the men returned, like the rest of Japan, to the Tokugawa shogunate's ban on Christianity.

The beast's distended belly, curving alongside Tokyo, holding the capital prisoner, recedes with a bow to Fuji-san and courses to the southwest, toward the monster's pelvis. The lower limbs taper off at Shikoku and Kyushu, the dragon's tail dragging the Ryukyu Islands. Our story is set within the pelvis of the dragon, in the part of the country known as Kansai. Here, on a latitude with Los Angeles and Casablanca, lies Osaka, crown of Kansai. Osaka—Japan's third-largest city, mercantile center, city of canals, Venice of the East. In Osaka is found the country's oldest temple, marking the introduction of Buddhism from the Asian mainland. *Osaka*, which Americans pronounce *oh-SAHK-ah*, comes from the Chinese, meaning *big slope*; slippery in rainy season.

Ginger O'Neill arrives in Osaka in July, by which time the heat has ripened the *suika*—watermelon—small and sweet in fields alternately muddy from rain and mud-cracked from heat, the heat climbing from below, from the earth itself, and dropping from above, from the sun. The farmer cleaves suika with his knife; he sucks its membranes for midday comfort. That sun—*taiyo* in Japanese—the farmer can't live without. It ties a person to it, to its life force, to life's necessity, to energy from the burning star, to energy from the dying star.

July in Osaka—the air is hot in the city and countryside, hot in the rice fields and hot in dazzlingly bright buildings where the air conditioning, by American standards, is set warm. The ground is hot—hot in dry, thin soil and hot in irrigated, fertilized dirt. Farmers feel the heat, sweating as they weed their rice terraces, sweating as they feed their vegetable patches, sweating as they pick their fields of tea, each pick, as the season progresses, lower in quality than the one before. City pavements are sizzling hot, and after-hours, when it should be cooler and people should be enjoying their vodka martinis and *junmai-shu*, there's scant cooling. Nighttime offers little break from the heat and humidity, the sun rising too soon for the darkness to bring much relief.

July in Osaka—families head for vacation in the mountains or in the cities or at the sea. The tourism industry anticipates one of the year's stellar intervals. These summertime school holidays are good for business, and business is cash. In Anno Domini 2000, Japan is on a cash economy relative to other industrialized nations, credit cards remaining in wallets, tucked away for big expenses like hotel bills. Neighborhoods are quiet, houses dark, office parking lots deserted, but trains are packed, highways jammed, swimming pools rowdy, tennis courts hopping, shopping arcades hectic, parking decks full, *pachinko* parlors smoky. Shrines, temples, resorts, and playgrounds find in this time their heyday, their days of hay and harvest, flowering of fields echoed in flowering of trade. Restaurants featuring sushi on conveyor belts hit record sales. Geishas' dance fans noiselessly lick at the coming dusk. Cormorant fishermen work at night, from lighted boats, in the traditional fashion. The summer has its charm, hot as it may be.

July in Osaka—life goes on. Farmers go on. Shopkeepers go on. Pensioners who can't afford to leave town go on. Unaffected by school calendars or by corporate holiday shutdowns, these Japanese wait through the heat and the sun and the rain for a different portion coming to them at a different time: autumn train rides to see the maple leaves, New Year's with family in the south, a winter ski trip to Hokkaido, a springtime cherry blossom pilgrimage.

Still other Osakans stay home through July because they are attuned to different academic calendars, different from the calendars of public schools. These are the Japanese who for philosophical or social reasons, not unlike their Western counterparts, enroll their children in private schools; they find themselves with shorter summer vacations, narrowing the possibilities for travel. With vacations two or three weeks shorter than those of the public schools, these expensive academies provide more value for the tuition-payer's yen in summertime. This extra class time is a feature of private schools that parents are willing to pay for, but it obliges teachers to contend with classes and exams through the intensity and distraction not just of the heat but of the high school baseball season. The teachers, moreover, themselves sleepy from summertime partying, must lecture around the more-than-usual sleepiness of upperclassmen, upperclassmen who are pulling all-nighters to study for university entrance exams still months away.

In these hotter than hot days, Japanese private school teachers greet visitors from abroad with apologies for the heat. Some of these teachers live in suburban Osaka, in middle-class tract houses, in neighborhoods built in the boom of the 1980s. They are Japanese people who, for whatever reasons, professional or personal, host a foreign man or woman for a short time. This foreign guest of theirs might never have visited the dragon before.

One of the things Ginger O'Neill has come to Japan for is the sushi. The problem is she isn't getting any.

For supper Hiro Murakami's wife, Sakiko, serves shrimp, eggplant, onion, and green pepper in the tempura style, battered and deep-fried. Ginger's lips grow greasy, and Sakiko gets up for a box of tissues, holding it out to their guest over the table. Sakiko has prepared the rice in her automatic rice cooker; the cooker bears an elephant trademark but looks like an igloo. The rice is eaten plain. Hiro is through his second bowl before Ginger has eaten a quarter of her first. The rice is tasteless and a little dry for Ginger. She prefers her rice with raw fish on top of it.

The Murakamis and their guest are seated on chairs in the dining room, nothing more than one side of the living room. Ginger's place has been set with knife and fork, in addition to chopsticks. Ginger refuses to touch the Western flatware. She asks her hosts about the low table and floor pillows in the room she saw down the hall.

"As a matter of fact," Sakiko says, "we use pillow room for traditional Japanese occasion. For American guest, chair is better."

Ginger had been looking forward to sitting on the floor. She says nothing, her mouth full of shrimp, her head full of her own preconceptions.

Sakiko is shorter than Ginger and rather long-waisted, and when Ginger picks up her tissue after it slides off her lap she sees that Sakiko's feet aren't touching the floor. Sakiko sits with her spine against the back of the chair;

she moves as if she once were a gymnast or dancer, her steps rhythmic and certain, her posture as upright as a marionette's. Hiro has poured Kirin for Ginger, himself, and his wife. Mai, a leaner version of her mother, sips cold wheat tea. Sakiko wants to know how Ginger's trip was.

"*Kanpeki,*" Ginger says. Before dinner Ginger had looked up *perfect* in her Japanese dictionary so she could use it to compliment her hosts, or at least to register her pleasure. Her trip wasn't really *kanpeki* and still isn't, for her suitcase remains missing. It has good resonance, though, *kanpeki* has. Ginger likes the sound of it. It's firm, final, the last word on the subject.

"*Kanpeki?*" Sakiko laughs. She seems surprised at the word. "What do you mean?"

"I mean it's perfect. Nice." Ginger is easily troubled about matters like language. Perhaps she used the word incorrectly.

"But if I lose suitcase, I cannot say trip is perfect. So, Ginger-san, how do you like Japanese food?"

"It's delicious." What can Ginger say? If she can't have sushi she might as well have tempura.

"Tempura is mother recipe. Sometime I think Hiro marry with me just for it." Sakiko pushes the tempura platter toward her husband. "Ginger-san, I cook lunch for you every day while you on assignment."

"I'm sure that won't be necessary."

"It is what I do. I do for husband every day."

"How? Where?"

"You didn't hear about Japanese lunch box?"

"Won't I be able to pick up something at school?"

"School doesn't sell food. Only give coffee and tea for teachers. You will make drink. My husband show you how."

Surely Ginger's not going to be the coffee girl. She's reminded of how the teenaged Reggie would let Ginger attend her parties only if Ginger fixed and served the refreshments. Ginger hated that, and it gives her an unpleasant feeling now.

Sakiko addresses her husband with a Japanese word Ginger doesn't catch. "You show Ginger-san how she get around teacher kitchen, neh?"

Hiro is feeling around in his shirt pocket. "I will have someone show her. One of the office staff."

"Someone show you how to make tea, Ginger-san."

"Where do the students eat?"

"At desks. They bring lunch too."

Quiet until now, Mai speaks up. "I love pork dumpling." The girl's accent is strong, and she strings the syllables together as if she's threading popcorn on a Christmas tree chain. "*O-KAA-san,*"—it sounds like a sheep's bleating—she looks at her mother, "you make pork dumpling?"

"Maybe."

"Your English is good, Sakiko."

"We studied English in school. I speak—no, no, I spoke English at job. I hope you correct me if I speak wrong."

"What job did you have?"

"I helped conference for foreigner. My husband didn't want me to work after daughter was born."

Hiro shrugs.

Sakiko gets up for the plate of melon on a table behind her. "Please, have fruit. Dessert." She hands the plate to Ginger. "Melon is gift from neighbor. We make fruit for gift because fruit expensive. We hesitate to buy ourself."

Ginger can afford to buy herself a melon regardless of the price but is old enough to remember her mother buying them at roadside stands for fifty cents apiece. She puts honeydew and cantaloupe on her plate. "Melon is expensive where I live too. Sometimes I pay four dollars for one."

"Cheap. For muskmelon we pay around thirty-six dollar, for one melon."

"How much?" Ginger is in disbelief.

"When my friend travel to States, she go to grocery store to see. Your melon cost little. *Ringo*—apple—expensive here also."

The kids at Confederate High toss whole apples from their lunch bags into the school's trashcans.

"What did you do to celebrate millennium?" Sakiko asks.

"The millennium?" Ginger lets melon juice trickle down her throat. The juice feels good now, but the honeydew will irritate her throat for hours after this, as if she's coming down with a cold. Ginger loves the taste and the sometimes squishy texture of the melon, though, so she eats it nonetheless. "I don't believe the millennium changes until the end of this year. Everyone I know thought the event was to be celebrated six months ago. My daughter wanted to go to the Mall, you know, near the Capitol in D.C."

"Good!" Sakiko says.

"I'd heard of a terrorist threat, so we didn't go."

"Some people in this country feel this too. About year millennium end. How old is daughter?"

"Sixteen."

Sakiko taps her fingers on the tabletop, translating the number.

"You could celebrate twice, Jinja," Hiro says, swallowing the last of his beer.

Ginger turns to the girl. "How old are you, Mai?"

"Sixteen." Mai looks at her watch. "Excuse me, Ginger-san, I go back to my books. I have much work." She picks up her dishes and leaves.

The Murakamis' home is smaller than Ginger is accustomed to. She feels conspicuous and intrusive of the privacy between parents and child. And this extraordinarily quiet daughter isn't anything like Bernie. Bernie entertains whoever will listen with wild and probably false stories about people at school; she impersonates her teachers, ridicules the administration. She speaks as if whatever she's saying is the most interesting thing a person could possibly hear. She *is* interesting to listen to, and beautiful to look at. She's a terrible student, though, to her mother's continuing anxiety.

Sakiko tells Ginger that even though Mai attends the school where Hiro teaches, she walks to the train station from home and arrives at school on her own each morning. Her father drives separately. Ginger will ride with him.

Hiro's gold-cased lighter makes a dry brush sound as he lights a cigarette.

"I tell my husband he shouldn't smoke, but he doesn't listen. His voice is changing from tenor to—what is word?" Sakiko frowns at Ginger.

"Baritone," grunts Hiro.

"*Hai*, baritone," says Sakiko. "She is dropping voice tone and she doesn't stop." Ginger doesn't correct the gender of Sakiko's pronoun, and in fact Sakiko's English is fairly efficient. She makes mistakes with verb tenses, pronouns, and number, yet she's perfectly comprehensible. English is full of unnecessary and bothersome rules. The rules create strata of speakers and writers, rewarding form over content and creating an educated class arrogant about its language skills.

"I smoked when you married me," Hiro retorts. Both he and Sakiko look cross. Sakiko says something to him in

Japanese. Hiro is silent. Ginger and her deceased husband had an understanding about not quarreling in front of company. They both hated domestic tension, whether displayed for others or privately nursed.

"I heard you humming an opera aria earlier this evening, Hiro."

"In youth I sang for fun, but I don't have time for it now."

"She spend all free time at manga shop."

"Manga?"

"Japanese comic," Sakiko explains.

Hiro drops his cigarette in the ashtray and stands. "Manga is much older an art form than people think. Excuse me, I have work."

"You see, Ginger-san, every night I am left with dishes." Sakiko looks self-satisfied.

"I'll help you."

The women load lacquered bowls, ceramic plates, and plastic, lightly textured chopsticks onto painted tin trays.

"Put things anywhere you find place. Japanese man doesn't help wife in kitchen." Sakiko is standing on her toes, groping in a cupboard, reaching to the back of a shelf. She pulls out a tall brown bottle and unscrews the cap. "Here, have drink. For health." She reaches for two glasses and pours a clear liquid into them. The women take sizeable drinks of the licorice-flavored liqueur.

"Ministry of Education put more emphasis on spoken English all the time," Sakiko continues as she loads the dishwasher. "We are happy to think of sister school in America." Then, "Mai expect—*expect*, that is right word? She expect you are tall and blonde."

"I was blonde when I was little. Never tall."

"Mai wish he is blonde. When you come, he, *she*, want to know English word for freckle. I look in dictionary."

"My freckles have faded."

"Mai like freckle. Me too. You look young. Cute."

"I was surprised to see all those golden-haired young people in the train stations."

"Crazy," Sakiko says. "As a matter of fact, our school is strict. No make-up, no hair color, no nail polish, but after school some girls put on make-up and paint nail. They take off polish next morning before school. Waste of time."

Ginger nods.

"And no dating," Sakiko adds.

"What?"

"At our school, student is not allowed to date."

"Each other?"

"No one."

"My daughter should do a school exchange here! She was so angry she wouldn't even kiss me good-bye at the airport—"

"Your daughter date a lot?"

"Not so much, but she likes her freedom. She was angry because I asked her not to date while I'm here. It seemed a small thing. She said it was like asking a married couple not to have sex for three weeks." Ginger had wanted to remind Bernie that her father was dead so her "no-sex" argument was wasted, but Bernie would have scoffed her teenage scoff. Ginger let her fume without giving her more arrows to shoot. "Does Mai mind not dating?" she asks Sakiko, trying to fit the leftover containers into the refrigerator, eyeballing what's already inside. Other people's refrigerators always look so interesting.

Sakiko seems elsewhere. "My daughter is sixteen," she says at last. "She knows studying at her school will help get in university. In less than two year she will take entrance exam. Exam is very difficult."

"My daughter goes to a private school, too. What does Mai want to study?"

"She wants to be a doctor. Doctor for children."

"An accomplishment to look forward to. My daughter wants to be an actress."

"Movies?"

"She's been in community theater since she was nine. She acts, sings, dances." Ginger doesn't say it, but Bernie was referred to in a local paper as a young Madonna. Ginger made copies of the column and mailed it with their Christmas cards that year.

"And your husband, Ginger-san?"

"I'm a widow."

Sakiko turns off the tap, twisting around in her slippers to face Ginger. "I'm sorry," she says, looking at Ginger's hand. "I see your ring. I think you are married."

"It's okay. It's been a while." But Ginger's stomach is knotty, the way it was when Sakiko and Hiro were arguing. Ginger didn't remove her ring within the year that Steve died. Then inertia set in and she couldn't make the decision to take it off. She doesn't like going over the story about Steve, and her sister tells her if she weren't still wearing her ring people wouldn't ask her about a husband. When people find out she's widowed, they're usually either tongue-tied over her loss or argumentative about how she gives a false impression. In either case, it doesn't take them long to get around to setting her up for dates.

"When did your husband die?"

"My husband die twelve years ago. I mean *died*."

"So long."

So wrong.

"Cancer?"

"Steve was killed in a tunnel collapse. He was chief engineer on a construction job. The digging didn't go as planned. One of the supporting beams buckled and he was buried." When Ginger got the phone call from Steve's boss, she couldn't see. She had her eyes open but she couldn't see. Everything in front of her was black. Ginger always says the same thing about her husband's death. It's too painful for her to think of new ways to express it, his dying, alone, no one to comfort him, no one to hold his hand to the end. It's the worst way to die.

"You miss him very much," Sakiko says. "That is why you wear wedding ring. You don't believe husband's death, even after twelve years. You wear ring to hold him." Sakiko speaks in a quieter voice as she wipes the cooktop with one hand and reaches for her glass with the other. "If you marry again you have father for daughter."

"He wouldn't be her father." Bernie asked for Steve in the days after his death, but her appeals tapered off as the weeks went by. "No, if I were to remarry, it would be for me, not for my daughter."

Sakiko is rinsing the sponge, squeezing the water out, letting it refill the cells, squeezing it out, again and again. "I would not marry if my husband die. Man support family and sometimes is friend for wife. Once retire, husband become wet leaf, stick to wife. It's difficult for wife to see friends after retirement."

Sticking to wife sounds biblical.

"As a matter of fact, Ginger-san, in Japan woman have more fun with friends. In America too?" Sakiko scrubs at counter spots Ginger can't see.

"I'm not sure," Ginger says, accepting a refill of the liqueur. "My husband and I were best friends."

"My husband is not best friend for me. But he is okay as husband."

"My sister lives near me, and together we've brought up Bernie."

"Together brough—"

"Together we've brought up Bernie." Ginger speaks more slowly. "Bernie's staying with my sister while I'm here."

"That is cute name—Bernie." Sakiko rubs her forehead with the back of her hand. "Not boy name?"

"Her name Mary Bernadette. Husband favorite name for girl." Ginger has already been around Sakiko too long. "We call her Bernie."

"Mary is common name in States?"

"Not so much any more, but our family has had many Marys. My sister's Mary Regine. My own name is actually Virginia Marie. And my mother was Maureen—an Irish form of Mary." As a girl Ginger wished she had a more fanciful, less ethnic name. A fun name like Wendy or Holly would have been nice. Or something romantic—something you could spin a good story from—Cleopatra or Lucretia, for instance. Anything but Virginia Marie, or almost anything—Pollyanna would have been worse. Ginger came up with her nickname at the age of twelve. She likes it but wishes it were androgynous like Reggie's. She compromised with Steve on Bernie's name—he liked its religious overtones; Ginger likes the nickname.

"Ginger-san, are you Catholic? Or Puritan?"

The anachronism startles Ginger, and she searches Sakiko's face for a joke, but Sakiko looks serious. "Roman Catholic," Ginger says after a moment, distinguishing herself from Anglicans and Episcopalians. Although these distinctions probably mean nothing to Sakiko, they mean the world to Ginger.

"Ah, Catholic," Sakiko repeats. "I had friend who was Catholic. She kicked out of church when divorced."

"Oh?"

"Husband left her for Korean woman. Why did your church cut her? She did nothing wrong."

Ginger doesn't know what to tell Sakiko about the Church and divorce. She can't get into the intricacies of Catholic marital law with Sakiko; Ginger can't figure the law out herself.

"Excuse me, Ginger-san. I should not talk about church."

"It's complicated."

The Church would not excommunicate Sakiko's friend for being divorced—it would consider her still married. A problem would arise only if she wanted to marry again. That's when she would have been *cut*, as Sakiko put it.

"Complicated," Sakiko says. She opens her mouth as if to speak, then closes it. She pours herself another drink and pushes buttons on the dishwasher. "You know, Ginger-san, my husband, she call you *Jinja*, but that is word for Shinto shrine. She is lazy about speech. She—*he*—want you to think now he works on lesson. My husband is playing computer games in your room."

Ginger laughs. "In America we say the only difference between men and boys is the size and expense of their toys."

Sakiko turns out the kitchen lights. "I try to say your name properly, Ginger-san. Now go and take bath. Mai prepares it for you. Guest is first."

"Thank you." Ginger knows an entire family will delay their bathing for the guest to go first. Ginger would actually rather shower in the morning, but that appears not to be the routine here at the Murakamis' house.

"I hope water is nice temperature for you."

Still later Wednesday

The bathwater was Popsicle blue and smelled like my laundry detergent. It was an odd experience for me, sitting there on that little plastic stool, my feet on the slatted wood floor. I soaped and rinsed using the showerhead and only then got into the tub to soak. Per Sakiko's instructions, I left the warm water for the rest of the family. I hope I left it clean.

Sakiko caught me on the stairs after my bath. "Ginger-san, do you like sushi? One night my husband may take us to sushi restaurant." Her face was even more flushed than it had been over our *après* dinner drinks. "If you like sushi," she said. "Some people don't."

"Sushi would be great." I saw my favorite food laid out before me: small, sweet grains of rice crowned with delectable raw fish. Then, remembering how people from home who've traveled here advised me that it's extraordinarily expensive to eat out in Japan, I added, "I can treat."

For a moment I thought Sakiko was insulted. Then she smiled. "I talk to my husband."

With her promise in mind, I checked my e-mail. The Murakamis have given me their third bedroom, a "six-mat" room that Hiro uses as a study, so I have easy access to their computer. Hiro showed me before dinner how to get to my e-mail. About the big red ball he uses for a chair, Hiro said, "It's good for your core muscles." What's this *core muscle* business? Sounds like physical therapy; more jargon trickling down to the layman. Some day our dictionaries will consist of nothing but technical terms laicized.

I had a note from Bernie and a note from Reggie. Bernie says she misses me and reminds me that Reggie gives cooking all her attention, unlike me, who plays the piano with one eye on the stove. The weather's been lousy—cool and rainy; still, having her own room and bath at Reggie's sure beats camp, she said. Not surprisingly, there was no apology from her for her airport behavior. Well, *I'm* sorry we parted after having words. I'll write and tell her that. Apologizing is not beneath me.

Bernie's not a bad girl, not really, she's a normal kid, although she spends too much time with her friends and not enough with me. Her friends aren't always the best influence on her. Last year when I was dating that bizarre dentist (the one who likes sushi because it's soft food, and he'll eat only soft food so as not to break his teeth), Bernie said I should feel free to have a man live with me. That was rich—my own daughter telling me I could shack up with someone, and as if I would have Dr. Dentin move in with me! If I were going to allow my values to go to pot it certainly wouldn't be with someone as uninspiring as Larry Dentin. In any event, it's not going to happen, so there's no need to speculate about how it would be with this man or that man.

Some of Bernie's friends have divorced parents (none are widowed like me, I'm a dying breed) with stay-over boyfriends or live-in companions. I just can't see it. I don't want to live with a man I'm not married to, especially not with a daughter for whom I want to set an example. Reggie says I use Bernie as an excuse to avoid intimacy. Reggie should talk. She becomes intimate but never commits.

Concerning commitments, or of wanting me to procure one, I also had an e-mail from Walk. He wants to be sure I understand just how important this sister-school thing is to the entire district, if not to the Commonwealth of Virginia and the entire D.C. metropolitan area. He might as well have said the future of the civilized world rides on my ability to get a *hai* from this Japanese school community. He reminded me that my three-week stay was requested by the Japanese principal, as a way to be sure everyone here is comfortable with the long-term, personal relationship we are entering into. Does Walk think I need to be reminded of that? Do I look like Simple Simon? He'd never admit it but there's a lot at stake for him in this—doesn't he think I can see that? Especially now that he's been publicly humiliated by his wife (soon-to-be ex-wife), he needs a win.

Reggie's e-mail reported Bernie is giving her trouble over curfew. She asked if I have suggestions. I said I make a point of staying up until Bernie comes in, no matter how tired I am. Sometimes I sit in the foyer, sometimes out on the front steps. That way Bernie knows I've been expecting her, worrying about her. I told Reggie it would probably work even better for her to do this because Bernie would be embarrassed about inconveniencing her aunt. The strategy assumes Reggie doesn't have a friend over with whom she's in bed, although I didn't say that.

I'm exhausted, but Sakiko's mentioning her divorced friend has me thinking. Sometimes I wish I'd been born into a less rigid, less demanding, less difficult faith. My creed is clear: I believe that Jesus is God and that He rose from the dead. Surely I can find a religion requiring from me nothing more than that faith. However, it's impossible, at least extremely difficult, for me to get past what I grew up with, and I'm not prepared to abandon the Catholic Church. I like the liturgies, the sacraments, the traditions that link me to my past. I like belonging to something bigger than myself, I like the universality of a community, and I like the pattern of convictions springing from an ancient time. Saint Peter's Basilica and the white-cloaked Pope represent the past drifting into the future, my life flowing forward and backward into time without end. My faith affixes meaning to eternity and to my life. It offers me hope for reunion with loved ones.

The Church doesn't make life easy for Catholics who've lost a spouse. If I had all the men in the world to choose from, that would be fantastic. I don't and it isn't. I can't marry a divorced man and stay in the Church, not unless the man's marriage has been annulled, and how can anyone count on annulling a marriage unless they're

Princess Caroline of Monaco or one of the Kennedys? Reggie tells me I should let myself fall in love and only then, if it looks like marriage is in the offing, deal with the Church's rules. That's way too risky for me. It's a good way to end up with a broken heart—having to choose between Church and the man you love.

I'll stick a petition for peace of mind in with my evening prayer. In any case, the marriage issue has nothing to do with this trip. I'll lose sleep about it some other time.

Thursday, July 6

My suitcase didn't arrive during the night. I've got just what I wore or packed in my carry-on. Sakiko ironed my travel dress last night, but otherwise things aren't going well.

There's no bathroom on this upstairs level, only what could truly be called a water closet—the tiny room has a toilet in it, no sink. The toilet bears puzzling controls, with many unidentifiable push buttons on a side panel of the seat. For all I know, it could be a space-saving bidet. I trust I wasn't supposed to use it for washing my hands. Anyway, not recalling how I flushed last night, I pushed the wrong button to flush and then didn't move out of the way fast enough. Shooting jets of water managed to soak my last clean pair of underwear.

After that mishap, I snuck downstairs in Sakiko's bathrobe to do my hair and make-up. Having slid closed the frosted glass door of the lavatory (which is what I'm calling the room with the sink—each room here serves only one function), I waited as the fluorescent light stammered and its blue notes bounced off the pink porcelain basin. The light accentuated the rosy tones of my nose. I looked like an old Irishman after a night of highball drinking. I washed my hair at the sink, mulling over the fact that Bernie hasn't gone to bed yet half a world away.

Plucking hairs from the bridge of my nose, above my right eye, then my left, I made a natural straight line into two arcs. The women in *Ran*, that Japanese cinematic *King Lear*, had no eyebrows. Tweezing is so time-consuming that sometimes I'm tempted to shave mine off and replace them with cosmetics. Here, if anywhere, it would work.

On went the SPF 130 sunscreen I found on a shelf next to the sink. Its initials and numbers gave it away. The rays here must be burning hot. I put on my usual pale foundation, then a new plum blush to ratchet up my cheekbones, and, finally, my pressed powder, to cover up the previous layers. I picked through my make-up case, black and white plastic with an Eiffel Tower zipper pull, and from my assortment of eyebrow pencils pulled out the soft brown one. Separating fine hairs with strokes of the little brush on the cap and thinking of Albrecht Dürer, I turned line into rhythm with the pigmented point. My arched eyebrows may keep the basset-hound look at bay and distract from my increasingly hooded eyelids. Today my mascara and shadow stayed in the case. My contacts still feel scratchy.

By the time I came back upstairs, flapping along in a pair of all-purpose house slippers (which Sakiko keeps rearranging at my door, positioning them in the direction I'll next step into them), Sakiko was banging around down in the kitchen, preparing our bento boxes. The aroma of cooking pork swirled upward with the bug-repelling incense that Hiro is burning on the patio. The sandalwood fragrance—itself unmistakable—sent me back to college days. "Are we camouflaging marijuana again, Virginia Marie?" the resident assistant on duty used to ask me, but it was always my roommate. I got by on second-hand haze. Today I'm wondering if my life can be summed up as a process of replacing illegitimate drugs with legitimate ones. I'm tense about appearing at the school this morning and have rattled my bottle of sedatives a couple of times. I don't want to be too mellow, though, and since I won't be on a plane, I shouldn't need them. Nervous energy may work in my favor for the assembly I'm facing.

The smell of Sakiko's cooking reminds me of the barbecued hog we ate crossing North Carolina years ago. Bernie and I had driven to Asheville to check out Thomas Wolfe's home, and we decided to take the slow route back to Virginia. Even in our air-conditioned car, windows up, I suffered mile after mile of sensory distraction along those back roads. The fragrances flashed snapshots before me—hickory woodchips cindering under hog smokers; black kettles binding the dryness of vinegar and the spike of garlic; brown sugar laying its sweetness overall.

My reputation is legendary: I'll eat anything. Bernie and I started sampling barbecued pork around Valdese and didn't stop until we reached Raleigh. Hauled into controversies at roadside barbecue stands, we became jurors in the trial of sauce versus sauce. Barbecue sauce with ketchup from western North Carolina competed for our love and affection with vinegar-based sauce from eastern parts of the state. Our voices drawl-less, we were "objective" tasters, until in a tractor-trailer-packed blacktopped lot I suggested to Bernie only half-facetiously that we were committing the sin of gluttony. Thereupon we abandoned our roles as hanging judges and sped north on I-95. Pulled pork had created a greasy mess on my favorite white shirt, orange smudges from ketchuppy sauces threatening to haunt me. Men and women who noticed my spots tossed stain-removal secrets at me over tabletops and cash registers, but once I was home I found nothing removed them. I still wear the blouse, hiding the stains with a pullover.

My few things I've laid out on the low table in the room, and I've found myself several times since I arrived in my old school-days position: kneeling. The ridges in the tatami mats are surprisingly soft, like corduroy, but for a couple minutes at most; then I have to sit. There's an odd odor about the room—either the mats are giving off a swampiness, or the walls are mildewing. Through the upholstered folding walls I hear Hiro humming "Nessun dorma" again. *No one's sleeping* is right. I'm punch-drunk from jet lag.

I've tried to translate temperatures from Celsius to Fahrenheit, multiplying by nine and dividing by five and the other way around—I can never remember which— and adding or subtracting thirty-two. I gather, more from what Hiro said yesterday than from my own calculations, that today Osaka is headed to ninety-five degrees, and that will be a humid ninety-five. Hiro says there's no air conditioning in the classrooms but the teachers' room has several window units. *Mushi atsui* they call the weather—hot and muggy. Sakiko and Hiro have muttered the expression several times since I arrived.

As I dressed, Sakiko's pantyhose remonstrated with me from the knee-high table where I'd left them last night. She'd handed me several pairs in a tangle, different sizes and colors of the devilish garment. I presumed I could go to school barelegged, given the climate, but Sakiko asked me if I needed stockings, since I'd lost my luggage. Actually, she *told* me I needed stockings; she was specific, even pedantic. "Women of our age, we dress up when we go in public, Ginger-san. Skirts and stockings." Her English was surprisingly complex. I wonder if the Confederate High School committee gave me this assignment because I wear skirts to school. Maybe they know more than I thought they did.

My foray into the Japanese stocking trade wasn't pretty. First I tried the pair closest to my skin tone. The crotch topped out at the middle of my thighs. As I tugged on the second pair I brooded over how the hair on my legs has grown so fast. I got the right leg twisted and found I was walking with my foot turned in. I took that pair off and started over but couldn't get it right. I settled on the hose that make my legs grass-green but have the most space. Japanese women have skinny legs. The hose look particularly bad with the bright linen dress I packed in my carry-on and that Sakiko ironed last night. I may be peeling the hose off at school, although that would be drafty, as I'm leaving the wet underwear behind. Sakiko couldn't lay her hands on her hair dryer and said she uses the clothes dryer only for emergencies. Everything else she hangs to dry. Apparently she didn't think this was an emergency. She said I could keep the pantyhose.

I could do with some sushi. *Toro, saba, ikura,* I can't get enough of it. I see it now, beautiful in its geometric shapes and abstract patterns. If nothing else about Japan works out, if I'm a failure at my assignment, I hope at least the food will make my trip worthwhile. I'd hoped today I would have a traditional Japanese breakfast like at the hotel.

On the patio, bug-free, in full view of my lace-trimmed panties on the line, Hiro and I had eggs, toast, and coffee. I asked if this was a special meal for me. Sakiko said it's what they eat every morning except on weekends, when she fixes French toast and sausage. Mai left for school as we sat down to eat. She looked like an American private school student in her cute if humdrum uniform. Sakiko was finishing up our bento boxes and stacking them in cloth, zipped bags of Black Watch plaid.

Hiro's calling. I've got to stop. I like this journaling. *Oops!*

Two

Tamago

Ginger-san is latching her seatbelt as Hiro dusts off his minivan's dashboard, turns control knobs in circles, and searches through his satchel for his clip-on shades. He backs out his truncated driveway in a rush, missing by inches both his neighbor's wall and an old man in a business suit. Ginger, in the process of applying lipstick, finds hot pink goop on her upper front teeth, courtesy of Hiro's sudden stop. The video screen on the dash warned Hiro of the wall and of the man, had Hiro minded the screen. The man is sweeping the middle of the street with a broom like something from a Colonial Williamsburg gift shop, the handle a birch branch, its corn-straw bristles tied with string. Street sweeping by neighbors is a delightful Japanese custom, but the custom has turned into a relic. The younger people aren't interested in it. It's good for tourism, though, except it's usually found off the beaten path, in ordinary neighborhoods where people like Hiro and Sakiko live.

"Today we are a little late, Jinja." Hiro drives with the windows open, air conditioning off. His glasses are slipping down his nose, already slick in the heat; his crew cut shows traces of gray. He's a Japanese version of Poindexter, from the Barbie board game. To Ginger he's a different person this morning than he was at dinner last night. He's talkative.

"I'm sorry," Ginger says. "By the way, what's the Japanese?"

"Eh?"

"For *sorry*. What's the Japanese expression for *I'm sorry*?"

"It's not your fault. I slept too long."

"But what's the word for *sorry*?"

"No need."

Hiro could be accommodating and tell Ginger the word she's looking for. She doesn't ask him a third time, she who buries herself in dictionaries, style manuals, and thesauruses. "I woke at five," she says instead. "Time-zone troubles."

"Five! You should go out and help the farmers!"

There are farm vacations in Japan, rather like working farm offerings in America, but Ginger is in the here and now. "Besides the assembly, what will I do today?" she asks.

"I will take care of you."

"Does your committee have meetings arranged for me?"

Instead of responding to his guest, Hiro makes a sharp left turn, narrowly avoiding two biking schoolgirls, their dark pleated skirts and white blouses rippling in the breeze. Ginger grips the bar over her seat. Her teeth are clenched, her jaw aching. She opens her mouth and sets her tongue between her front teeth to relax her jaw. That helps relieve the tension, but if Hiro hits a bump, Ginger will bite her tongue.

From her passenger's seat on the left side of the car, with every turn Ginger fears Hiro is veering into the wrong lane. The first time she visited the British Isles, until she got used to the reversed roadways, Ginger thought she'd surfaced out of a cold pond into a matriarchal society. Women drove most of the cars, the men their passengers, their captives even. It seemed, if only for moments, that men had given up command of the cars, that women, shorter but stronger, had seized control of the social order. The fact is Ginger had been looking in the wrong seat. Now, again, she's confused enough that if someone gave her directions, she'd translate a right turn into a left.

Something else is troubling Ginger, for she wants to do the right thing.

"Sakiko calls me Ginger-san. Should I be calling her Sakiko-san?"

"She's being respectful."

"She's lovely."

"I'll say something to her."

That wasn't where Ginger saw the conversation going, but she drops it.

At the next cross street Hiro points out a discount bookstore but admits there aren't any books in it that Ginger could read. It's a good thing she packed several for herself, to help pass the quiet evenings she's expecting to have. Evenings back home in the study of her handsome Colonial Revival house, Ginger snuggles up with her books. Many of the volumes that interest her are out of print, so she acquires them second-hand through specialized catalogues or, more recently, over the Internet. The books every now and then arrive with yellowed and brittle pages. When she opens the books, no matter how old they are or where they've come from, Ginger sniffs the cracks between the pages, smelling tobacco, mold, and other less familiar odors. Some of her favorite books are about opera companies from the time that excites her, the bridge years at the end of the nineteenth century and beginning of the twentieth. The earliest photographs of staged opera productions hint at a heaviness, at space closing in on the performers. The elaborate sets somehow seem top-heavy, and Ginger—although she knows better—looks at them with wonder, half expecting the flats, the props, and the people themselves to tip off the page and into her lap. Moreover, the air in the sepia photos is dusty, something it wouldn't be if the same pictures were colored. And so the photos possess a certain spirituality: Ginger can't look at them without seeing ghosts hovering in the background. For her the link between that time and the present is tenuous, the moments not on the same continuum. Indeed, that time and this are two unrelated, isolated points in the ether, a hole dropped into the timeline before the First World War, before the modern era.

The streets are clogged with cars, but Ginger and Hiro make progress. The urban-suburban landscape is sprinkled with skyscrapers, strip plazas, tiny storefronts. At a convenience store wedged between two high-rises, Hiro parks the car and gets out, leaving the engine running. He returns shortly with a pack of cigarettes and a plastic container of sushi. *Tamago-yaki*. Japanese omelette. As he maneuvers back into traffic, he opens the sushi box and offers Ginger a piece.

"Use these chopsticks if you want. Or your fingers." He peels the chopstick paper for her with his teeth. "To tell the truth, I like the way you licked the sauce from your fingers at dinner last night."

One piece of sushi—Hiro eats the rest of it—is more satisfying to Ginger than Sakiko's fried eggs and toast.

They pass a medical center, two train stations, and several housing developments before they pull into the school's parking lot. Hiro parks at the far end of the lot and heads up the hill to the school. Ginger must run to keep up with him. Her legs make a swishy noise as her stockings rub together. The painter Paul Gauguin liked the fleshy legs of Polynesian women. To him thin legs on a woman looked like tongs. Ginger's certainly not fat, but no matter how slender she is at any given time, her thighs rub together. Gauguin would have loved Ginger's voluptuousness.

Three middle-aged men in white shirts and dark trousers have congregated at the bottom of the school steps. As Ginger and Hiro approach, two of them are blotting their foreheads with neatly pressed handkerchiefs. This morning Hiro is the big man on campus, for he is in possession of the Visitor. The men direct their glances at Ginger. After exchanging morning greetings with his colleagues, Hiro gets around to introductions.

"*Hajime mashite*, Ginger O'Neill *desu*." Ginger practiced with Hiro on the way to school. She bows as the men speak to her in a combination of Japanese and English. They're wearing the same thing Hiro is—dark slacks, white shirts, dark ties. They bow to her. More conversation, more glances her way. Ginger might have been better off not wearing her dangly earrings on the first day. She might have been better off with the holes in her ears showing.

Finally Hiro turns to Ginger. "The head of the history department says you have nice Japanese manners."

"*Arigato gozaimasu.*" With her *How do you do?* and her *Thank you*, Ginger has run out of Japanese words, save those that have to do with food. Words like *o-toro*—honorable tuna—and *ika*—squid—our scholar has learned from eating in Japanese restaurants over the years, using as language texts both menus and Asahi beer ads tented on tabletops.

At the top of the steps is a man standing alone, holding a violin case. There's something almost menacing, animal-like, in his posture—shoulders broad, chest full, hips narrow, a tiger on the prowl. His eyes rest on Ginger's until she looks away. He reminds her of Ken McMillan, a student at her high school for a semester when she was sixteen. Ken had a Japanese mother and an American father. He appealed to most of the girls and took a special liking to Ginger. They had a few dates. And while what they did together is nothing compared to what kids do these days, Ginger still thinks sometimes about how she shouldn't have been doing it. It felt too good.

In the entrance hall, Ginger takes from her bag the school slippers Sakiko lent her, tucking her street shoes into an open cubicle. The halls are filling up with purposeful-looking high school students dressed in white shirts or blouses, navy blue slacks for the boys, navy skirts that fall just below their knees for the girls. Each pair of white crew socks rises more or less to the same place on the girls' calves. The boys wear inside slippers of standard-issue navy blue plastic, the girls red. All the students whose eyes she catches bow to Ginger.

The man with the violin case brings to Ginger's mind the last night she and Ken were together, back when Ginger's senses would easily overtake her reason. On that night, in a deserted park out by the reservoir, a policeman found Ginger and Ken tumbling over each other on the grass. They saw the officer late, when his flashlight shone in their eyes. He knew most of the residents of Lockton and recognized Ginger. As Ginger grabbed her clothes, the policeman explained that his concern was for their safety. He wrote both their names on his notepad. Ginger didn't know if he'd file a report or if her parents would get a call. She worried about it for weeks, was sick to her stomach whenever the phone rang, until enough time passed that she figured it was a moot point.

Reggie, that year a freshman at the university, was happy when Ken moved away. She had warned Ginger to be careful about him; his appeal was evident even to her, a sophisticated college woman. Ginger and Ken lost touch after a year of passionate letter-writing. Ken has been on Ginger's mind lately.

Because of the way Ken looked and the way this man looks—is it the shape of their faces? the way their lips simultaneously pout and play up at the ends?—Ginger found herself, there on the school steps, wanting to see him up close. She was warmer than the Osaka morning accounted for, and she was disappointed that they were not introduced.

Later Thursday

From across the stage I couldn't catch the eye of the principal as he sat erect in his gray business suit, his hands flat on his thighs, so I squinted beyond the floodlights and into the audience. The hush was a world apart from the usual racket at Confederate where small groups of students keep up a chattering hum through the course of every assembly. If I win this school, these polite people will think Americans hopelessly rude.

Hiro said he'd be nearby during the welcome ceremony, but he disappeared behind the plush red stage curtains. The announcer's Japanese went on and on and I became uneasy, wondering if I'd missed my cue. I liked hearing that voice, though—low, dreamy, poetic, pausing briefly at what seemed like ends of lines, lingering as a musician might at whole rests here and there. I caught myself falling into a trance and could only hope I would notice even a butchered *Ginger O'Neill*. I trusted my name would stick out like an electric guitar in a nineteenth-century orchestra.

When I did hear my name, I was startled at the American Midwest sound of it. For a moment I wondered where I was. Standing and tugging at my dress to flatten the skirt, I was glad for once to be wearing hose so my dress wouldn't be sticking to the back of my thighs. I rose and crossed the stage, bowing to the principal and the assistant principal, as Hiro had told me to do. Then

I took the podium. Hearing only white noise, I suddenly felt deaf. Impulsively I reached for Sakiko's pearl strands. They felt like Mother's rosary beads.

I glided through my speech, my slippered feet unconscious of the stage's wooden boards. It was exhilarating—as though I'd been lifted into the air. I was an eagle above the crowd, keeping watch on hundreds of sable heads. Public speaking always intoxicates me, even here, perhaps especially here, where I'm not entirely understood.

Song-mi had helped me with my speech before I left Virginia—it was mostly in English, but I had wanted to dot it with Japanese. Maybe I'm naive, but I trusted her not to include anything embarrassing, a Kennedyism about being a jelly doughnut, for example. There was no laughter, which I took as a good sign. In fact, the applause was enthusiastic.

At the end of the principal's remarks, the student body president entered the stage from the wings and presented me with a Titanic bouquet of roses, daisies, and hot-house lilies. He led me down the stage steps and up the center aisle as the ovation continued, and on to the principal's office for a reception. I felt like Queen for a Day.

Waiting to meet with me in the principal's office were a handful of English teachers and twice as many students, one boy and one girl chosen by each teacher. I don't know how they got there before I did. We were served orange juice and rice crackers by administrative assistants wearing uniforms that looked like flight attendants' circa 1980—coordinating blouses and skirts done up in a mint green twill. They had on bronze-hued hosiery.

I gulped my drink, the orange pulp knobby on my tongue. The boys lined up to meet me, each telling me he wants to do business in America. One said he liked my remarks at the assembly, especially the part about the different classes he could attend if he were to do an exchange at Confederate. He spent five minutes telling me about his father's import-export business, using good vocabulary and sentence structure but terrible pronunciation. He kept accenting the wrong syllable, like jee-oh-MEH-tree. I had to ask him to repeat everything. He told me three times he plans to establish a branch of his father's business in Oh-MAH-hah.

"Why Omaha?" I asked, once I realized that, no matter what the word was, he accented the penultimate syllable.

"The steaks," he said, and he winked at me as he walked away. Japanese people aren't as undemonstrative as I'd thought.

Once the boys went back to class, one of the women teachers—in slacks, open-toed shoes, no hose—led me over to the girls. They wanted me to speak to them in Japanese. I tried to convince them I don't speak it. They giggled. I could feel Hiro's eyes on me as he encouraged the girls to go back to class.

Before lunch I sought out the washroom. On its threshold sat a row of pink plastic slippers, so I stepped out of my school slippers and into the pink ones on the way in and back into my school slippers on the way out. All the toilets were the squatting kind. It seemed a problem with the hose. I ended up taking one leg off before I used the toilet. That sounds odd, as if I had a removable leg. The washroom smelled of urine.

A row of blue plastic slippers waited outside the boys' room. What's with this pink-blue dichotomy anyway? It baffles me that disparate cultures can be stuck on the same color distinctions for the sexes. I always want to give blue clothing to girl babies and pink clothing to boy babies, although I can never bring myself to follow through with pink for boys. I don't know why people color-code their children. Bernie's never been partial to pink. It's a flattering color on her, but she doesn't like it. Every time I dressed her in it as a baby, which wasn't often, she threw up on it.

Hiro had a meeting during lunch, so he left me at a desk in the vast teachers' room, where there's row upon row of desk after desk. The teachers all have their offices in the same room, no dividers, no cubicles. The desks touch each other on three sides. Because the students don't seek out the teachers, apparently, the traffic in and out is manageable. My desk belonged to a woman Hiro said was fired. He fixed his eyes on the empty chair for a few seconds after he told me that, but he didn't say more.

I counted three women out of fifty teachers in the room. They were sitting at desks several rows away. They weren't wearing uniforms, unless tailored clothing in muted colors is a uniform. I felt out of place in my more casual, by now wrinkled dress. The reddish-orange stood out like a bonfire on the beach.

I looked for the man with the violin case but didn't see him. The men on either side of my desk teach math, Hiro told me before he left me between them. They didn't speak to me. Thinking they might respond to written English, I wrote *Hello, my name is Ginger O'Neill* notes to them, and they wrote simple *Hellos* back to me. I couldn't see continuing this way. I needed both my hands in order to eat.

Sakiko's hand-packed lunch was delicious. It's too bad the plastic *hashi* she included were smooth and slippery, though, because eventually I lost control. I dropped a pork dumpling in my lap. The math teachers pretended they didn't see, but the teacher whose desk touches mine, front meeting front, laughed out loud. I hadn't paid attention to him until then—he's old and wrinkled and looked nearsighted, given the distortion his oversized lenses gave the sides of his face. Hiro hadn't introduced us. I smiled at him and nodded my head, picked the dumpling off my lap with my fingers, and ate it with excessive gestures of lip-smacking. The old teacher laughed again, wrote something on a square of creamy paper, and pushed it across his desk onto mine. I've kept it. It says, in a jagged hand, *Welcome.*

THREE
Curry Rice

Tonight, on the heels of his success directing Ginger through the welcoming ceremony, Hiro has a staff meeting. In other words, he's going to a bar with his male colleagues. Ginger has not been invited.

With Hiro out of the house, the dinner hour is more relaxed. Sakiko serves curry rice, a heavy, spiced beef concoction, a traditional meal in Japan, notwithstanding its origins in India. Sakiko pours a dry French wine. The wine is meek, not standing up to its dinner companion. Mai puts the glass to her lips but doesn't drink.

"*Kare raisu* is my husband's favorite dish. Sometime I cook his favorite meal when I know husband goes out. I'm a bad wife, neh?"

Mai eats quickly and excuses herself.

"You had busy day, Ginger. How was welcome assembly?"

71

"Delightful. You treat visitors better than we do."

"Visitor is very important person. But does your daughter study as hard as my daughter?" Sakiko asks, using English pronouns properly. The fact that she's on to a new topic is frustrating to Ginger, for whom the welcome assembly was worth talking about.

"Bernie barely studies."

Sakiko looks up from peeling an orange. "And you are serious person."

"I may be, but my daughter wastes her talents. She waits until the last minute to do her assignments, crams with Cliffs Notes, stays up all night with classmates working on group projects. I don't know how she'll get into college."

"American university is difficult to enter?"

"It depends on the school. But Bernie isn't sure she even wants to go to college. She isn't concerned about what happens if the acting jobs don't come her way. She's so different from me."

"My husband tell me teachers ask what you like."

"What I like?"

"What you *are* like."

"And?"

"I wish I do interesting thing with my life. Like you, Ginger, you have exciting life, teaching, traveling."

Ginger opens her mouth to respond. Sakiko cuts her off. "I am typical Japanese housewife. Yes, I have what I need, but I'm hungry for something more."

"What?"

"I like to work with color."

"I noticed you've decorated with orange and violet."

"They are colors of sunset in Nagasaki. My home as child."

Nagasaki. Why does Sakiko have to be from Nagasaki?

"It's never too late to get started in a career," Ginger says, at a loss for what to say about Sakiko's childhood home.

"What about you, Ginger? Do you realize your dream?"

"I like my job, although I wouldn't mind something more creative." Ginger imagines herself in a garret, bent over a typewriter, a cashmere scarf keeping her pretty neck warm, stacks of books zigzagging in aisles across the chilly room.

Sakiko plucks an orange seed from her tongue. "Ginger, do you know, when Japanese woman marry, her name removed from real family record and added to husband family?"

Ginger composes a picture of a green-eyeshaded bureaucrat in white shirtsleeves and black armband, seated high on a stool at a counter, razor in hand, cutting through names on a ledger.

"I had no idea."

"Wife become part of husband family. Not member of own."

"What happens when a couple divorces?" Ginger asks, but Sakiko's on her feet and carrying dishes to the kitchen. Ginger follows her, accepting Sakiko's licorice-flavored drink again, on ice tonight.

"Sakiko, I'm wondering if you can help me. Do you think we could find someone who lives in Osaka?"

Sakiko sails out of the kitchen and back in with a phone book.

"Do you mean Osaka Prefecture, or Osaka City, Ginger?"

"I don't know. Southern Osaka, I heard."

"My book covers some of cities in southern Osaka. We should try to find this person. A friend?"

"Someone I went to school with."

"Japanese?"

"His mother's side."

"Family name?"

They find *Makumiran, Kenta*. This was easier than Ginger expected.

"Do you want to call him, Ginger?"

"I don't know." Ginger shuts the book, Sakiko barely freeing her hand in time. "I'll think about it."

From: Reggie Conway, Esq. (taxlit@anonymail.com)
Date: Thursday, July 6, 2000 9:36 AM
To: Ginger O'Neill (sushilover@mailforall.com)
Subject: Progress report

Ginger,

Sounds like you're having a good time on your mission.

As for Bernie, she came in late last night and was late for school today. Partially my fault. I overslept. To be honest, I wasn't exactly sleeping. Jeff, that guy I met at the Corral last week, spent the night. Don't worry—Bernie didn't know. She was out when he arrived and we were extra-quiet this morning. Practically had to put a sock in my mouth, though. Won't write more. You never know where e-mails go!

Getting Bernie off to school isn't bad, short term, but I don't know how you put up with that bell schedule all year. Starting school at 7:20 is uncivilized. Why don't you quit your job? You could write or something. You certainly read enough. How's it going with that blank book you took with you? Any hot prospects to report in it? Can't wait to read! Just kidding! Anyway, you could write for the *Post*—opera reviews, maybe, for kicks.

Got to run. Tax law is hell. The IRS is blowing down my door.

Reggie

From: Ginger O'Neill (sushilover@mailforall.com)
To: Bernie O'Neill (flybaby@mailforall.com)
Subject: Dying for sushi

How was your day, Bernie?

My suitcase that was lost finally arrived today. I'm afraid carrying it upstairs may have given Mr. Murakami a hernia—I offered to take my clothes out downstairs so he wouldn't have to lug so much weight up to my room, but he waved me aside and dragged the trunk behind him up the steps. The steps are pretty steep, and actually this evening I slipped down the last few—am having some trouble with the slippers I'm wearing around the house. I wish the Murakamis had carpeted their steps. Not that I wouldn't have slipped on a rug, but it wouldn't have hurt so much when I did. I'm okay; my tailbone is just a little sore, especially when I'm sitting on the big red ball, like now. Mrs. Murakami was alarmed at my fall. When she asked me if I was hurt, I said no, just my pride, which she didn't get so I explained that expression to her. She wanted to run me to the emergency room, but sitting on the sofa with a bag of ice behind me for a half hour had me feeling a bit better. I like Mrs. Murakami a lot. She's funny and interesting and a good cook too.

They had a lovely welcome ceremony for me today at the school. You wouldn't believe how well-behaved the students here are.

Aunt Reggie says you've stayed out later than we talked about. Please be considerate of your aunt. If you want to dodge curfew, wait and do it after I get home.

I'm dying for some sushi. It seems just out of reach.

I love you.

Mom

FOUR

Aji

The corridor ends at the music room. Yoko, one of the uniformed women in the front office, gave our visiting teacher directions there when she asked if she could use a piano. Ginger showed Yoko the music binder and dribbled her fingers along a phantom keyboard on Yoko's desk. *"Pee-ahn-oh,"* Ginger said. Yoko smiled and drew a map of the path from the office to the music room, then escorted Ginger out the office door. Pointing her down the hall, Yoko purled along in Japanese as Ginger began her walk, trying both to bow and not to turn her back on Yoko. Yoko stayed at the office door, propping it open with the heel of her foot and bowing back at Ginger, waving to the American until she rounded the first corner.

As she drifts down the final hallway toward the small, dark opening of the music room, an opening that looks hardly big enough to squeeze through, Ginger is put in mind of Lewis Carroll's Alice. From time to time, the imagination can overtake the rational mind, flouting the laws of perspective. Sometimes, now being one of them, a person might fantasize what her life would be like if her senses controlled her. The wise individual doesn't give in to those strange thoughts for long.

Although carpet spans the floors in the school's modern addition, this older wing is laid with linoleum, linoleum that has become honey-colored from waxy buildup. After school the students here get down on their hands and knees and wipe the smooth floors with rags; the carpeting they thwack with finger-bands of masking tape, harvesting lint, crumbs, hair. The hallway smells of dust from thousands of steps taken across it. How much flaking skin, how many eyelashes have fallen to the floor? The dust in the air and on the ground is a dust both of the living and the dead, for what is dust but proof of those who walk among us now and of those who have gone before?

The music room is a regular classroom. Instead of desks, though, it holds a piano, a gleaming black concert grand. The piano shrinks the classroom to childish proportions. As if she were unwrapping a present, Ginger folds back the fall board and reveals the creamy keys, their soft color inviting her, tempting her to them. She opens the lid, choosing the half stick.

Ginger's still wearing Bernie's favorite nail polish, Fiji Lilac, which now looks garish and ragged. Bernie had been applying it for her mother the night before Ginger's trip. It was then Ginger had mentioned the no-dating rule. Bernie had stormed off, leaving Ginger to paint the nails on her right hand herself. The right hand looks even worse than the left.

Before lunch today, Friday, end-of-the-week for American schoolteachers but not for Japanese, Ginger met with science teachers about curriculum. They asked her many questions about sequencing of topics in the lab sciences. She was out of her depth, having course syllabi for her school's offerings with her but no experience with the material. She ad libbed and sounded convincing even though she fabricated a lot of what she said. After lunch Hiro told Ginger she looked tired. He suggested she take a break. Ginger had packed her music binder for the trip and had it with her today just in case she were to get access to a piano. Lady Luck is with her.

So our pianist, no less passionate about music because she's an amateur, not professional, musician, seats herself on the bench and opens her music binder to a Schubert waltz, the pages heavily marked with Ginger's reminders of accidentals. She has studied this piece assiduously. The waltz is in B, beginning in the minor and ending in the major, a cloak wrapped around itself and closed with a sparkling brooch. The dotted rhythms make the treble notes nearly equal in value. As for the chords in the left hand, they are basically inverted triads. Ginger plays the piece three times, increasing her familiarity with this instrument, judging its key and pedal responses. She hums along.

Next on the program is "Song of India" from *Sadko*, which Rimsky-Korsakov wrote for a tenor. Ginger's piano arrangement of it belonged to her grandfather. The tune is of course more Russian than Indian. Ginger's left hand plays the arpeggios *piano* while she moves the right-handed melody along in the same dynamic. As the inner voices in the treble fade to *pianissimo*, the right hand becomes like two people at once, like a child gaining adulthood, a child emancipated, who finds his increased freedom brings with it increased responsibility. Ginger concentrates on striking the keys rhythmically, with just the right pressure.

Her second time through the song, Ginger discerns activity from the corner of her eye and is aware she's not alone. With a tipsy, diagonal strut, a red-brown crustacean draws near her, and Ginger lifts her feet to rest them on the pedals. A crab scoots under her skirt, heading for the window wall.

"Are you enjoying our national wildlife?"

The crab surprised Ginger; the voice startles her. Ginger looks over to the doorway. Standing in it is the man who was at the top of the school steps yesterday, the man with the violin case. Ginger recovers any composure the crab may have robbed her of. "Like the crabs of my summer vacations," she says, "but they were *outside*."

"Rainy season. Crabs don't know inside from out."

Ginger looks for the crab. It's gone.

"North Carolina?" the man says.

"What about North Carolina?"

"Did you summer there?"

"We spent a week at the Jersey shore each summer."
Hours of reading in the car until they reached the water.

"Do you live in New Jersey?"

"Me? No, in Virginia." He's grilling her, like a fish.
"How about you?"

"What about me?"

"Did you grow up in Osaka?" Ginger is pitched to
the man's dark eyes.

"Where in Virginia are you from?"

"Nether Gorge, outside D.C. You ask a lot of
questions!" His parrying would drive many women mad,
but Ginger has met men more challenging, more insistent,
than this one. The truth is he excites her, intellectually.
Some other part of her being is aroused as well.

"I could be an American." The man laughs and moves
closer to Ginger. "Pardon me, I haven't introduced myself.
I'm Sato Akira. Sato is my family name. Please call me
Akira." His high, angular cheekbones, long nose, golden
complexion, and squared-off chin make him look almost
American Indian. "And, yes, I did grow up in Osaka."

The man walks around the piano, and Ginger sees
that his hair is pulled into a ponytail with a black elastic
band.

"I'm Ginger O'Neill," Ginger says, rising from the bench.

"I know your name," he says. He is slightly taller than she.

"You were at the assembly?" She takes his offered hand, his flesh soft and warm. His eyes stay on hers long enough to make her draw back.

"I introduced you at the assembly yesterday, Ginger."

Now she recognizes the voice—the low, broadcaster's intonation. "Excuse me. I should have caught that. I'm happy to meet you. Where did you learn to speak English?"

"My mother translated English poetry, and I spent hours as a boy listening to radio broadcasts of English lessons."

"I hope I wasn't disturbing you with my practicing."

"Not at all. I was in the hallway enjoying the Schubert, but your Rimsky was even more moving. You make good phrasing choices."

"You recognized the pieces?"

"I'm the music teacher." He straightens his tie. "Welcome to my studio."

"I didn't know anyone would be—"

"No problem. I have a theater in the new wing. That's where I hold most of my classes."

"Hiro, my host—but you must know he's my host— he told me he thought I could play on a school piano, and the woman in the office gave me directions here. I didn't know it belonged to anyone in particular." Ginger reaches for her binder. "I'm not a professional musician."

"It doesn't take a professional to play with expression," Akira says, stopping her by laying his hand on hers.

"I'm sure that's right."

Akira has withdrawn his hand and is moving to the far side of the room. He stands with his back to the windows. Ginger narrows her eyes to look at him.

"Anyway, the piano isn't my primary instrument," he says. "I'm a singer. I studied at the conservatory in Cincinnati. Know it?"

"I've heard of it. Did you like Cincinnati?"

"Japanese food was hard to find."

"I'll bet there's plenty of sushi there now."

"You like sushi?"

"Sure."

"I'll take you out for sushi, but right now I have an appointment. I'll be in touch. It was nice meeting you, Ginger O'Neill." He disappears into the hallway.

"And you," Ginger calls out to where the man had been. Was he asking her for a date? Akira is his first name, but what's his last name? Soho? Santo? Satiro?

Ginger takes her seat at the piano again and turns the pages in her binder. The next piece is "The Glory of Love," from *Guess Who's Coming to Dinner*. Its lyrics are light and trite weighed against that movie's premise. Ginger is unhappy to see it among her more serious pieces, unhappy she brought it with her. She gets to her feet and rummages through the papers in the piano bench, discovering some sheet music, a Western transcription. As she picks out the melody, she recognizes it as a traditional Japanese song. She heard it at a performance of the Koto Society during last year's Cherry Blossom festival in the nation's capital. On the koto, a long zither that sounds quarter tones, the koto's notes falling between the piano keys, the song was spare and delicate, like Amy Lowell's poetry or a ripe persimmon; the tones were fugitive, fleeting, like life. But on the piano the piece is monotonous, imparting none of the wraithlike twang of the Eastern instrument. Ginger tries some chords as accompaniment, achieves a muddle of sound, and closes her binder.

Ruminating on the prospect of a sushi meal, Ginger can feel the fish flesh cool and heavy in her mouth. She tastes the vinegared, sweetened rice of *nigiri-zushi*. She sees the tongue-shaped delicacies in their hues of pink, white, and silver. She even smells *aji*—oily horse mackerel, one of her favorites—and she can only hope it's in season.

FIVE
Suzuki

On their way to dinner Saturday night, Hiro is like a boy on a go-cart—his restless foot on the accelerator producing abrupt starts, followed in turn by sudden braking. He seems to be making turns for no reason other than that he can, and Ginger has suspicious moments, supposing this a wild ride without end.

"Ginger, do people in States use *navi* system?" Sakiko asks.

"Where are we?" Ginger wants to know.

"New car has GPS," Sakiko says.

Hiro didn't use GPS to or from school. He watched game shows on the way home. Ginger doesn't mention this to Sakiko. "Where are we?" she asks again.

"We are fewer than three kilometers from home." Through his mirror, Hiro directs his comment at Ginger, takes a long drag on his cigarette, inhales, tilts back his head, and blows the smoke into the fabric ceiling of the car. Ginger considers the blackness of his lungs.

By the time they arrive at the restaurant, Ginger is queasy from the smoky air, the corner turns, and the uncertainty of her whereabouts. The steamy parking lot wilts her, and she feels like the spinach in a wilted salad, or, in fish terms, like poached sole. The heat and humidity are worse than on the Potomac, worse than those oppressive summer days and nights in Nether Gorge when Ginger won't leave her centrally air-conditioned house, even for sushi. The sound system in the restaurant gushes perky Japanese music, fizzy and syrupy, the female vocalist high, flighty, and artificial. The recording sounds stuck, the song never getting anywhere, like some reggae music that Ginger would like if it weren't so repetitive— same melody, same rhythm, same chords over and over again. Even Puccini's ingratiating melodies would be an improvement over what's on this system, as would Andrew Lloyd Webber's predictable tunes.

In alcoves around the edges of the room, men, women, and children have removed their shoes and are seated on cushions on the floor. Ginger and her hosts, though, are shown to a square table and hourglass-shaped wooden chairs in the middle of the room. Hiro folds his paperclip frame into the curves of the seat, and Sakiko, once seated, stretches her neck, like a bird, craning her head from side to side. She's either working out some stiffness or looking to see who's here. Under the table Ginger slips off her shoes.

Hiro engages in an extended colloquy with the waitress, taking notes in pen on the palm of his hand. The place setting of disposable chopsticks is enveloped in white paper, stamped red and black with an *ukiyo-e* print of a woman, her mouth open to show off her tongue between her teeth. The one-time use of the chopsticks is a disappointment to our American; she thought she'd find reusable ones in a restaurant in Japan. After all, one doesn't eat with disposable cutlery in a nice American restaurant.

"What do you think about Japan?" Sakiko wears a pleasant if slightly astonished look once she has applied her evening makeup.

"I think Hiro works hard. The days are long for your teachers. School on Saturdays is something we don't have in the United States, even for half a day. By the way," Ginger continues, less at ease, "I'd like this meal to be my treat."

"That's not necessary, Jinja. The principal wants you to have a good time here. Tonight we are on the school's expense account."

Sakiko gives Ginger the thumbs-up sign. "We can go shopping tomorrow. Sunday is good day for shopping."

"I'm not much of a shopper, but I do need souvenirs for people back home." Ginger might as well get the shopping over with. Then she can read.

"My husband will take us shopping."

"I like the textiles I've seen in shop windows on the way to school."

"You would like to see *sashiko*, Ginger. Traditional Japanese cloth. I know place—"

Hiro clacks his beer glass down on the table and clears his throat. "Sato-*sensei* wants to take you to Kyoto tomorrow." Hiro is looking at his wife but isn't speaking to her.

"What did you say?" Ginger says.

"I said," Hiro says, turning to Ginger, "Sato Akira asked me to take you to the train station tomorrow morning at eight."

So *Sato* is his name.

"Why the train station?"

"He wants to take you to Kyoto. Cultural capital." Hiro wrinkles his forehead.

"Akira wants to take me to Kyoto? He mentioned sushi, not Kyoto."

Sakiko laughs. "They have sushi in Kyoto, Ginger."

"How far away is Kyoto?" Ginger searches her mind, trying to picture her map of Japan on the wall of her study, but all she can conjure up is blue. "When will we be back?"

"Kyoto isn't far, Jinja. You'll be back on the evening train."

The waitress lays on their table a platter of sashimi, a tableau. Fish slices, the size of domino tiles, sit on a bed of grated daikon radish, the radish acting as a lacy white bed sheet for the fish. After joining her hosts in an *Itadakimasu*, humbly receiving their food, Ginger picks up a piece of yellowtail and spreads fresh wasabi on it. The green, finely grated root resembles the reconstituted, artificially colored paste that Ginger gets in the States about as much as a horse resembles a mule. A direct hit of wasabi is staggering, like a whiff of ammonia. Dabbing it on a fainting person's tongue would do the job of smelling salts, yet wasabi is pleasant to eat if you're prepared for it. Ginger is trying to focus on the slice of raw fish, but she's hearing Akira's deep voice and seeing his thick ponytail.

Sakiko may be thinking the same thing. "Isn't he good-looking?" she says. Her rapid hand and chopsticks, flickering from the platter to her plate to her mouth, have Ginger transfixed. "You know he married, neh?" Sakiko adds, her mouth full.

How could Ginger have known that? How would she have guessed? She didn't notice a ring on Akira's hand, the warmth of which she now feels on her own. Since Steve's death Ginger has accidentally dated several married men. They hadn't shared their marital status with her, and she didn't know about their wives until it became obvious, like when, at a movie theater, she ran into one of them (a man she'd met in the drinks line during an opera intermission) with another woman. That man didn't wear a ring. Ginger asked about his movie date the next time the man phoned her. He admitted his marital status but said he thought it wouldn't matter to Ginger's feelings for him. Ginger hung up on him.

But is this a date or merely a cultural outing for teachers?

"I know nothing about Mr. Sato except that he teaches music at your school. I wonder what gave him the idea I'd go to Kyoto with him."

"You are American woman by yourself," Sakiko says.

"So?"

"He thinks you open to new experience."

Ginger can't tell if Sakiko's joking. She decides to take her comment at face value.

"Sakiko, it wouldn't be typical in the United States for a married teacher to take an opposite-sex colleague off to see another city, alone."

"Typical? No?" Sakiko squeezes her eyes shut. "I cannot tell his mind."

"What will his wife think?"

"Maybe she used to it. Eat! Please!"

They eat. Two minutes pass.

"Do you know her, his wife?" Ginger asks.

"Megumi," replies Hiro, sucking a slice of pink sashimi into his mouth. He motions the waitress. His wife nods to people at a nearby table.

"Do they have children, Akira and Megumi?"

Sakiko finishes chewing. "No children. Megumi-san has cosmetic business. She work for large Japanese company making demonstration at *depahto*." Sakiko pinches strands of daikon with her chopsticks.

"*Depahto?*" Ginger is herself picking up curlicues of carrot and radish.

"You use chopsticks well, Jinja."

"I've eaten Japanese food for years. I've been intrigued with chopsticks since I was a child."

"Department store," Sakiko says. "Megumi-san arrange display in fancy shop too. I like your hairdo."

The hairstyle from hell. Ginger changes hairdressers every few months. "I told my new hairdresser I wanted it short for the trip," Ginger confides, "but I'm afraid it makes me look like a boy."

"It makes you young, not like boy."

"We called it a pixie when I was little."

"I had pixie when I was girl. I miss simple of it. Of childhood too."

"*Simplicity*," says Hiro.

Sakiko glares at her husband. "You use special shampoo, Ginger?"

"You wouldn't believe how I choose shampoo. I stand in the hair care aisle of the supermarket and unscrew each bottle cap until I find one with the best smell."

"What smell?" Sakiko asks.

"Coconuts."

Hiro scrapes his chair on the tiled floor as he adjusts his position, moving neither in nor out, but sideways to get a better look at Ginger, or at her hair. He pours Ginger more beer as the waitress sets down a glass plate of sushi. "I need to call *Sensei* this evening, Jinja, to tell him your decision."

Ginger's on the train already, and it's a run-away. She looks at Sakiko. "Would you go if you were I?"

"It's only one day. Akira-san is very polite," she says.

"What will the school think of my going to Kyoto?"

"Often staff take visitors to historic sites," Hiro says. "Sato-*sensei* is on the committee for the school partnership. It's up to you."

While Sakiko's entire face is flushed, only Ginger's nose is red, reminiscent of a famous portrait of Franz Schubert in which the tip of the composer's nose is several tones darker than the rest of his face. Perhaps he was enjoying a few drinks while sitting for that portrait.

"Have some suzuki, Jinja. Sea bass."

The sound system is dealing out better music. The singer is Andrea Bocelli. Ginger is wishing she were home with her family. She's off kilter in this strange, East-West country. Bocelli's songs sweep along in a way Ginger has never noticed before—each beginning like a mountain stream, gathering speed as it meets other waters, tumbling over falls and resolving into a larger pool. Ginger's eyes sting around the edges, her nose growing tight at the bridge. Such are the physical effects of denying one's tears.

The conversation turns to politics, but Ginger doesn't say much, her lips numb from the beer. Hiro orders another round of food. He tells Ginger to try the *koya-dofu*—dried tofu and turnip skin. It sounds awful but Ginger likes it. They settle into a routine. Soon Ginger has that agreeable feeling of having had just enough.

"Is sister like you, Ginger?"

"She's entirely different."

"She is teacher too?"

"She's a lawyer, a tax specialist."

"Younger?"

"Two years older than I am."

"She has no family?"

"Just Bernie and me. Reggie's never married."

"Everything is okay at home?"

"Bernie's staying out late. She has school to get up for."

"Ah! How nice your daughter study this summer!"

"She failed chemistry."

The waitress brings *temaki* sushi. "Jinja, eat some eel," says Hiro of the fish and rice wrapped in dried seaweed, rolled into the shape of a cone. "This is the last course. Unless you are still hungry."

Ginger eats the *temaki* because it tastes good, not because she needs it. Between bites she tells Hiro she'll go to Kyoto with Akira in the morning. She stuffs her feet, swollen from salt and alcohol, back into her shoes. "I need to phone my sister and daughter tonight. Is it okay if we stop on the way home so I can buy a calling card? I promised I'd call them once a week."

"We can stop," Sakiko says. "Good idea to call."

"I'll need to get up early. I'll set my alarm, but I have a habit of turning it off without waking up. You won't let me oversleep?" Ginger's already worried about missing the train.

"Yes," says Hiro.

"Yes?"

"We won't let you oversleep, Jinja. You'll be awake in time."

Ginger was warned the Japanese answer negative questions literally. She inspects Hiro's face. His eyebrows angle sharply downward toward his wide mouth. He looks in some way crestfallen.

Saturday, July 8
Dear Bernie,

E-mail and phone calls are speedy and efficient, yet wouldn't you agree there's nothing like a piece of mail swishing through the slot, resting on the foyer rug, waiting for you, there to open when you get home from school? Maybe you don't appreciate it now, at sixteen, but, when you're older, you may think back to moments when you spied an envelope with your name on it, in a familiar and beloved hand. You may wish to have a moment like that again, a moment when you know someone thought of you, for yourself, not to hit you up for a donation to charity or to attend a home merchandising "party," and not to bill you or to send you insurance proceeds. No, I mean a piece of mail that you receive because someone wants to visit with you, a visit that you will attend to slowly, carefully, and then, after enjoying the visit, you will leave the letter on your desk or dresser for some little while, later slipping it into a cardboard box and placing it on a shelf in the spare room. When you have children of your own you may take it down and share it with them, or not, as you like. That is what I'm thinking of now as I'm writing to you. That and how much you enjoy seeing stamps from foreign lands.

I don't know what stamps you've received on this envelope, Bernie, for Sakiko has been kind enough to mail my letters while I'm out of the house—at school, or sightseeing. She has been so kind to me. I feel we'll be friends for the rest of our lives. *Someday you may have a chance to visit Japan and, I hope, to meet Hiro and Sakiko and Mai. I don't know if you and Mai would find much in common—her English is fairly elementary so you might want to learn some Japanese in order to talk to her—but for your mothers' sakes you could try to get to know each other. You, Bernie, are young and have that facility with languages youth enjoy, plus the gift for foreign tongues you were born with. Mai has many talents—she gets As in science and math—but English isn't one of them. Her mother, on the other hand, loves to speak English to me, and she wants me to help her with her vocabulary and grammar. I've noticed some small improvements in Sakiko's English even over the few days I've been here. I've seen basic English language books lying around the house, but I'm not sure they are Sakiko's.*

Enough of my trying to arrange things for you. But speaking of arranging, did you know there are still arranged marriages in Japan? Not many—more among my generation than yours, and there were more still of course among the older generations. It's hard for me to imagine what it would be like to have something as intimate as a marriage set up for me. Can you imagine it? Can you imagine being married at all? Your father and I were so happy together. I thought we'd see each other's hair turn gray.

The boys and girls at the Japanese school are much more polite than the kids at Confederate are, or at your St. Mary's even. They bow to me, and they don't call out rank words in the hallways. I could get spoiled here. Evidently there was quite a competition to host me. The Murakamis, as well as the other families who wanted to host, had to go through interviews with the partnership committee, even though everyone already knew everyone else. The Murakamis were chosen, Sakiko said, partly because of Hiro's rank and partly because Sakiko is home during the day. I'm sure she's being modest and that other, more personal things, went into the committee's decision. The Murakamis are lovely. And Hiro's English is excellent. He did a year of postgraduate work at Michigan State.

Bernie, I feel a little guilty about it, but I'm having a wonderful time. Tomorrow I'm going to Kyoto with one of the other teachers from the school, just a day trip. Kyoto is the cultural capital of Japan, and I'm expecting a beautiful city, like Paris, but with shrines and temples instead of churches. I will think of you and Aunt Reggie tomorrow and wish you were with me.

I must get ready for bed, so I'll close. I miss you terribly and wish you were here. I know that's corny, like what someone would write on the back of a postcard, written by a person who couldn't or didn't make an effort to think original thoughts. It's true, though, you know, my wishing you were here. That's how most clichés get started, by the use, then overuse, of a perfectly good and expressive saying. Did you know the word cliché is onomatopoeic? It comes from the sound a printing press makes, cliché, cliché, as it hits each paper to print it. Each paper is like the one before it, with no variation, no new thought.

Give my best to Aunt Reggie. And be good. Both of you!

All my love,
Mom

P.S. I'm sorry we parted at the airport under such strained circumstances. I feel terrible about it and wish it had been otherwise.

Six

Ikura

The way mothers sing to their children at bedtime, Ginger finds her lullaby in books. Tonight she cradles Graham Greene, her chest acting as the book's prop, her eyes intent on black and white, until she sees the same sentence pass her, again and again, one letter blurring into the next and the next. She turns off the light, rolls onto her side, and closes her eyes. In her sheer nightgown and Sakiko's heavily perfumed body lotion—Hypnotic Poison, by Christian Dior—Ginger notices in her body a sensuality she has overlooked, even evaded, in all her years of widowhood. There's something hard to account for about this time and place that makes her feel this way.

The house's other dwellers, possibly asleep, possibly attending to needs other than sleep, loom beyond the walls. The partition between her room and Sakiko and

Hiro's bedroom is a portable one, a sliding wall, a wall that can be drawn back to create one large room from the two smaller ones. Ginger can't help but listen in on the couple in the bed on the other side of the partition. She labors, against her conscience, to hear their intimacy, to hear if they speak of her, of Akira, of Megumi. She struggles to hear if they enjoy each other the way she and Steve did—those light sounds beginning with one of them and taken up by the other, until together, rhythmically, they sounded as calling birds, uttering their cries more and more in concert until they were one.

Not hearing anything but snores, Ginger finds herself awake in her misery, in her loneliness, and in her sin, if she were to acknowledge it, of being an *auditeuse* (although Ginger doesn't recognize neologisms unless she's come up with them herself). Much as she might not want to confess it, she would have continued to invade her hosts' privacy, if there had been anything worth hearing. Her examination of conscience will have to wait until she's ready to make it.

In her head Ginger plays a children's rope-jumping game: "A, my name is Annie, I'm from Albania, and I sell Adrenaline," through the Roman alphabet, all the way to "Z, my name is Zelda, I'm from Zaire, and I sell Zinnias." That takes less than three minutes on the bedside digital clock. On her back and studying a crack in the ceiling, Ginger composes haiku but loses track of the words as she counts syllables, so she fantasizes a fashion show for women in their forties. Finally, on her stomach, her ample breasts rounded, notwithstanding her weight on them, Ginger silently says two decades of the rosary, counting Our Fathers on her toes and Hail Marys on her fingers, at the last *Amen* praying for help in getting to sleep. She thinks over her decision to go to Kyoto, ultimately rationalizing the excursion as occurring in the ordinary course of business, a necessary evil, if it's an evil, to win the partnership. But isn't it hypocritical, and therefore doubly damning—for the offense and for pretending it's not an offense—to pray for the calm of sleep in a storm that one's own weaknesses have created?

At three o'clock Ginger wakes up hot, her room air conditioner having cycled off, and she punches it back on with the remote. At four o'clock she's cold and tugging at the cotton blanket. At five she hears the rain stinging the corrugated metal roof and thinks her hair will frizz, only to remember she has very little hair, and then worries her alarm won't go off. Ginger lies awake, thinking about Steve, and about Ken, and about Akira, until the alarm chirps at half past six.

Leaving her wretched hosiery aside, Ginger pulls on black linen slacks and an emerald green cotton shirt. She knows now she should have brought dressy slacks for school instead of skirts. The other women teachers wear skirts with hose, or dress slacks without hose. In Virginia Ginger teaches in skirts—she likes the romantic look a skirt bestows, imagining as she dresses she's Anna

Karenina or Emma Bovary—but never nylons when it's hot. A practical woman would shop today for slacks, but Ginger has a commitment that overtakes practicalities. Besides, she hates the tedium and randomness of shopping. Not only that; it takes time away from her books.

Hiro makes his way clumsily around the kitchen. Sakiko set the coffee up last night; this is her day to sleep in. Silently he and Ginger have their coffee and toast. Ginger feels uneasy about missing Sunday Mass and resolves to find a Catholic Church next week.

On the way to the station, Hiro hums "Gloire immortelle" from Gounod's *Faust* and points out the various sushi bars along their route. Ginger's favorite sushi restaurant back home sits in a red brick storefront at the end of a short row of shops in Nether Gorge. A few years ago the Noguchi brothers bought the small building, which had been used as a real estate office. They knocked down the interior walls and installed picture windows along the street, screening them with paper to let in the light but not a view of what Ginger calls the "filling" station across the street. Ginger likes to sit at the sushi bar and talk with Tatsuya Noguchi, his dark bangs hanging over his white headband, his tanned fingers pattycaking warm rice.

Akira is waiting for Ginger on the apron outside the train station. The music teacher is dressed in faded jeans and a denim shirt; he looks younger than he did in his school clothes, although his face is lined. He's leaner than

American men his age. Akira opens Ginger's door and offers his hand for Ginger's descent to the pavement. He smiles at her through the earpiece of the reading glasses dangling from his mouth. Brandishing the rail timetable, Akira tells Hiro they'll be back at nine.

On the train Ginger and Akira sit facing each other, their knees nearly touching.

"How is your trip going?"

"Frankly, I'm feeling a little silly about what happened last night."

"What was that?"

"I have a cousin in California. Yesterday—or is it today?—anyway, I wanted to give her a quick call to wish her a happy birthday."

"Sounds good."

"I figured that if Eastern time in the States is thirteen hours behind Osaka time, then San Francisco, being three hours closer to Japan, must be only ten hours behind."

"Ah."

The refreshment girl, in an antacid pink uniform, bows as she enters their car with her trolley. Akira buys two iced coffees.

"So I phoned Patty before we left for dinner at seven, figuring it would be nine on Saturday morning for her. But I'd miscalculated. It was three in the morning."

"You forgot the International Date Line."

"She didn't say that. She called me a name I won't repeat and slammed the phone down."

"Everyone makes mistakes, Ginger," Akira says, and, when he smiles, Ginger too finds humor in the episode.

The mountainsides along the route are soft and coniferous, a series of soft parabolas, echoing the shape of hands folded in prayer. In the young Rockies, where Ginger has skied, the trees look like pins crowded into a pincushion, pressed by God's palm to a uniform length. Their outline is steeply angled, the hillsides of trees forming severe diagonals. These Japanese mountains are more comfortable for Ginger, more in line with the ancient Alleghenies, the foothills of which she grew up in.

"This is your first trip to Japan, no?"

"*Hai.*"

"Good! You're learning the lingua. What's your favorite itinerary when you sightsee? Museums, shopping, nature walks?"

"For their architecture and art, churches are typically where I start," Ginger says, then is a bit embarrassed. "But of course not here."

"Where in Europe have you been?"

"Berlin, Vienna—"

"Have you been to the Vienna Woods? To Heiligenkreuz?"

"I have."

"Did you see the organ Schubert composed on shortly before his death?"

"I did, but I went to Holy Cross to see the monastery's architecture. Those odd bulbish domes—they made me think of Russia."

"You've been to Russia?"

"Just in books and movies. Oh, and operas. I've seen *Boris Godunov* eleven times. But what did you think of those low ceilings?"

"I was intent on the organ."

"I loved the monastery's arches," Ginger says, "and that rib vaulting and those stained glass windows—did you see those? Did you notice all the different abstract patterns in the windows?" When Ginger gets excited about things like this, her speech speeds up.

"Do you like Schubert, Ginger?"

"My taste runs to later in the nineteenth century. I make an exception for him, though. How did you guess?"

"Schubert," Akira says, "of religious and sentimental songs."

The organist played "Ave Maria" at Ginger's wedding, and Ginger laid one perfect white rose at the foot of the statue of the Blessed Mother. She and Steve knelt at the side altar together, their fingers, their hands, interlocked.

"But we were talking about stained glass—have you seen the stained glass at St. Hedwig's in Berlin?"

"You know, Ginger, Schubert probably died of complications from syphilis."

"His music stands for itself," Ginger says, ignoring the oddity of the turn in conversation. "He didn't need to be a saint to write good music, religious or not."

"That goes without saying, but did you know Schubert refused to include a portion of the creed in the sung text for some of his Masses?" Akira strains at the cigarette pack in his chest pocket, tugging at the fabric of his shirt. No smoking is allowed on the train. "Are you familiar with that line in the Christian creed, the one about one holy, catholic, and apostolic church? What do you think, Ginger, of Schubert's choice to keep that language out of his compositions?"

"Nothing in particular," Ginger says, although she hadn't known this about Schubert and doesn't know what she thinks about it. "Why, what do you think?"

"I'm not Catholic. It doesn't worry me."

"What religion are you?"

"Shinto by upbringing. I'm not observant. My parents weren't either, not really, but all four of my grandparents were, so out of respect my parents brought me up to know the religion."

"What about Buddhism?" Ginger is aware that many Japanese people practice both Shintoism and Buddhism. She wonders if that would be like practicing both Christianity and Judaism.

"No Buddhism. I'm only interested in religion as an intellectual pursuit."

Ginger leans back in her seat. She takes her eyes off Akira and looks around the train. The Japanese are easy on the eyes. They've no astonishing features—no grotesque noses or protruding eyes or vast bellies. Americans' looks are often bizarre, but Ginger, used to drawing mental caricatures, finds the Japanese hard to make fun of.

"What music do you like to listen to, Ginger?"

"When I'm grading papers I almost always listen to Bach. I know where he's going, and that allows me to concentrate."

"Structure helps a person know where he is."

"And you? What do you like to hear?"

"The Russians. Shostakovich, especially. Do you know his 'Waltz Reminiscence'?"

"Not off hand, but the Shostakovich I've heard is certainly stimulating, almost alarming."

"I like to be stimulated."

"I do too, but was Shostakovich always thinking of war and totalitarianism when he wrote music?"

"Probably," Akira says. "Still, I know what you mean. He is dramatic."

As the train nears Kyoto, the green landscape fades to drab concrete. The cultural capital had sounded to Ginger like something out of a fairy tale, but she sees now how homely vast areas of it are. Wan concrete mid-rises, in dull ochres and umbers, mix with flat, low, wooden boxes. A mass of power lines forms an overhead grid that, like wrinkles on a sunbather, doesn't flatter the city's complexion.

The couple negotiates the train station's vertigo-inducing escalators and boards a city bus. Except for the long seat across the back, the other seats are for only one person, so Akira suggests that Ginger sit next to the window on the right, in the long back seat. He slides in beside her and outlines their itinerary. They're headed uptown to tourist sites.

After a few minutes on the bus, Akira lays his right arm across the upholstery behind Ginger, not resting it on her but on their seatback instead, and, as more and more people board the bus, he leans forward and lays his left arm across the seatback in front of her. He has managed to imprison her. He looks closely at Ginger, then out the window, back and forth.

"What's your favorite opera, Ginger?"

"*Norma*." Ginger is beginning to realize this trip is more than a colleagues' outing.

"Bellini was a contemporary of Schubert, but he edged his way toward the Romanticism of Wagner and Verdi. A very dramatic opera, *Norma* is," Akira tells her.

They get off the bus at Nijo castle. After walking the gardens, Akira proposes they tour the castle. The floors are made of wood, and Akira explains the intrigues the shogunate plotted there. In their bare feet the couple makes the "nightingale" floors squeak. The purpose of the squeaking floors was to warn the occupants of intruders.

"Ginger, did you know the nightingales you see in America aren't the same nightingales we have here in Japan?"

"I can't say I did know."

"You should read Tanizaki's story 'The Portrait of Shunkin'—the blind heroine is fond of nightingales and larks."

"Whose story?"

"Tanizaki Junichiro. You may be familiar with his novel, *The Makioka Sisters*. About a Kansai family. It's been adapted for screen." There was never a tour guide more suited to Ginger's complex of interests.

"I'm not familiar with it." Ginger searches for a title that might appeal to Akira. Years ago she taught a book about an opera singer. "I don't suppose you've read *The Song of the Lark*, by—"

"—Cather. It was popular among music majors in America. An interesting book even though it bogs down," Akira says.

"I'll have to check out Tanizaki. Do you have other recommendations?"

"I have many. If you're reading Tanizaki, look for *Some Prefer Nettles*."

"Contemporary?"

"Nineteen twenty-eight."

"Odd title," Ginger says. "What's it about?"

"A man thinking of divorcing his wife."

Outside the castle grounds, they find a bench on a side street. Akira opens his canvas backpack and from it draws a thermos of cold tea, two plastic cups, and cold, processed fish on plastic sticks. The sticks have been manufactured to look like bamboo. The fish tastes sweet and clean and brings to Ginger's mind the Last Supper. The fish has become an American symbol of Christianity, but the pictogram Christians like to bolt to the rear ends of their cars looks as much like an open-ended infinity sign as it does a fish.

"You've been lucky so far with the weather. Rainy season hasn't been very rainy this year," Akira tells Ginger.

"I wouldn't have known that the night I arrived in Tokyo. I thought I should have come over in an ark."

They finish their lunches on the bench, then board the standing-room-only bus to the Golden Pavilion. Kinkaku-ji is a Buddhist temple, Akira tells his companion. Its three stories were built in three different architectural styles.

"The original structure of the pavilion was erected in the fifteenth century," Akira says. "What you see here is a replica of the building that was burnt to the ground in 1950 by an obsessed Buddhist acolyte."

Ginger sees what looks like a toy house on the far side of the water, the building framed by pillowy pines and shadowed by their dark undersides. The mirroring pond, surrounded by trees, reflects a heart-shaped sky.

"Do you have a book to go with this place too?"

Akira steps to the side of the path to let a group of German tourists pass. "I wasn't going to say anything because I thought I was overwhelming you, but since you asked, the classic story is Mishima Yukio's *The Temple of the Golden Pavilion*."

"That sounds familiar."

"The author was as disturbed as the man he wrote about. He committed ritual suicide upon completion of his last book."

"I'm going to have to start taking notes. The older I get, the less I remember."

"You are young, Ginger."

Ginger is quite a bit younger than Akira. Sometimes she feels old, though, as if the best parts of life have passed her by.

The couple walks on to Ryoan-ji, the Zen temple of the Peaceful Dragon, its dry rock garden raked to suggest a body of water, boulders evoking island outcroppings. They spend a few moments on the terrace overlooking the scene, then find places at a low table where two women in kimono serve them bitter green tea, swished to a froth in deep bowls. The tea's astringency is cut with sweet cakes made of red beans. The cakes are served with two-pronged, ivory forks on diminutive plates.

To enter the premises Ginger and Akira had taken their shoes off and left them on a shelf. Now, preparing to leave, they sit on a stone bench to put their shoes back on. Akira is finished before Ginger and walks ahead. Ginger adjusts the straps of her sandals and hurries toward Akira and the gate, when a crunching sound breaks the temple's stillness. Ginger is trapped among the stones, walking in the raked garden itself rather than on the pebbled path next to it. She takes her shoes off once more and picks her way toward the exit, twisting her face as rocks stab the soles of her feet. With as few steps as possible she makes her way back to the stone pathway. "Forgive me," she says to Akira, her guilt over etiquette a proxy for her deeper guilt about being with this man; by this time she is thinking forbidden thoughts of how it would be to kiss his lips, to hold his body close to hers.

"A mere peccadillo. And I'm sure you're not the first one to do it. Are you tired, Ginger?"

"I'm okay. Are we heading back to the station now?"

"I thought we'd transfer to another bus for the ride to Fushimi Inari Taisha, the fox shrine. You up to it?"

"There's a lot to see here. More than for one day."

"Who knows when you'll get back?"

Ginger nods. She can rest on the bus. "Why is it called the fox shrine?"

"The fox is a messenger from the god of grain."

At the fox shrine, Ginger looks at the hillside and commands her legs to move. Akira holds her elbow as they pass through the entrance and along the side of the gift shop, where chains of colorful origami paper cranes flutter before them in the breeze. Scores of traditional Japanese gates create shadowed tunnel paths. Akira's touch is a gentle guide.

"Torii are at the entrances to Shinto shrines. There are over two miles of gates here, one after the other, just a few inches apart. This shrine has ten thousand gates."

"Will we walk through all of them?"

"Not if you don't want to."

"Let's try a few."

The repeating pattern of torii, each of two vertical poles topped by a cross beam, invites them uphill. The gates are painted a warm vermilion with a hint of cadmium yellow. Their rhythm is reminiscent of Cezanne's large bathers, clicking by with their red heads.

"What color do you call the torii?"

"Orange."

"I mean in Japanese."

"*Orenji.*"

The ride back to the train station is crowded. A group of American kids—high-school students—sits at the back of the bus, taking up more seats than they need, while other people—male, female, young, old—stand in the aisles. The kids' chaperone, a middle-aged American wearing glasses and a baseball cap, tells the kids several times to give up their seats. They pay no attention to him. A few boys and one girl call each other obscenities. The loudest boy is tall and blond and blue-eyed, like Steve, but Steve never spoke like that. The words are ones Ginger hears at Confederate, but they seem miserably out of place here in Japan. Maybe the students think the Japanese don't understand the words. Maybe the students don't care if the Japanese do understand them. Ginger doesn't say anything on the ride. It's unlikely she'll appear Japanese, even in sunglasses, but she could pass for a European if she's silent. Akira doesn't speak either.

"See anything you like?"

The couple is standing in front of a narrow restaurant in the underground mall near the train station. Ginger points to a pretty sight in the window, the blue and white china bowl of *ikura-don*, plastic food for show like one can find in restaurant windows all over Japan. Ginger can't take her eyes off the glistening, bright orange globes, a jellied mass of salmon roe, *ikura*, on a bed of rice.

"What's been the highlight of your trip to Japan so far?" Akira asks when they've been seated and he has placed their orders for ikura-don.

"It's hard to point to a single thing as a highlight," Ginger fibs. Akira has been the highlight. "There's been so much I've liked."

"Maybe the food?"

"Am I that transparent?"

Akira stretches out his fingers on the tabletop. "You're an adventuresome eater. Sometimes visitors won't try our traditional dishes. It's fun to be with someone who's willing to try new things."

"Do you always take visiting teachers sightseeing?" Cupping the warm soup bowl in her hands, Ginger whirls her miso soup, shifting the currents of blond broth. Tendrils of green onion float on top; bonsaied cubes of tofu drift to the bottom. She raises the dark wooden bowl to her lips and swallows, the salty warmth sliding down her throat.

Akira shakes his head. "We don't get many. Who introduced you to sushi, Ginger?"

"My husband." Leaving no space for a response, Ginger adds, "Your national treasures are thoughtful places. I like that."

"There are more places I can take you."

Ginger is concentrating on the realities of this day, trying to avoid the fantasies. "Listen, let me treat you to this meal. You've been so kind, and I want to reciprocate." Is the school footing the bill for this trip? She wasn't asked to pay her train fare. Or is Akira paying for it? If so, what might he expect in return? Ginger's diplomatic skills only go so far here—and they are keeping her from asking too many questions.

"Absolutely not. When I go to America, my friends there won't let me spend a dime."

Ginger is fumbling with her main course, giving the lie to Hiro's compliment of her chopstick handling the night before. "When were you last in the States?" she asks.

Akira takes a bite of caviar and rice. "Two years ago I spent some time on the West Coast. How do you like your fish eggs, Ginger?"

Ginger has just put roe and rice in her mouth. She nods, swallowing the soft, brackish glob. "It's delicious. I'm glad you said to get the quail egg on top. But I must be making a mess of myself." The raw egg is sticky on her lips.

"I like watching you eat." For Mr. Sato, this woman is more than a colleague.

They wash their dinner down with Asahi Dry. Akira asks Ginger if she enjoys sake.

"You mean salmon? I love it."

"No, the drink, not the fish." Akira picks up the beverage menu the waitress has left at his request.

"I've had sake once or twice, but I didn't like it much, so usually I have beer with Japanese food."

"Has your sake been served warm or cold?"

"Warm. Why?"

"The best sakes are usually served cold."

Akira motions the waitress and speaks to her. She comes back with two glasses and a green, screw-top bottle. Akira opens the cap and pours a colorless liquid into one of the glasses. He hands it to Ginger. The glass is cool. "Smell it," he says.

Ginger can almost feel the alcohol in her blood stream as she draws in the vapors. "How much alcohol is in this?"

"Enough. Take a sip."

It's refreshingly cold and just hinting at sweetness, unlike anything she's ever drunk. "Am I supposed to be able to taste the rice it's made from?"

"If you drink it with your taste buds open."

Ginger nods.

"What do you think?"

"I think it must be an acquired taste, and I wouldn't mind acquiring a taste for it." She pours a glass for Akira, having learned from Sakiko that this is the polite thing to do in company.

"Your blouse picks up the lovely green in your eyes, Ginger."

Akira's compliment stirs Ginger in a way that feels both new and old. If she didn't know better, Ginger would think this man was making love to her. She forbears from responding.

After dinner, Akira buys Ginger an *uchiwa* at a kiosk in the mall. A woman's face, peeking over her own fan, decorates the front of it. As they walk, Ginger says she'll take it to outdoor summer concerts back home. She tells Akira about the time Reggie got her pocket-sized, battery-driven fan caught in her bangs during a summertime, outdoor performance of the community orchestra, just as the guest cellist launched into the thematic statement of Tchaikovsky's "Rococo Variations."

"I would like to meet your sister. Is she like you?" Why does everyone ask that, even in foreign countries? Reggie's dates always want to fix Ginger up with their friends, as if Ginger were anything like Reggie.

"Not really."

"She lives near you?"

"She moved near me when her job brought her to the D.C. area. She's a lawyer. Very smart."

"*You're* very smart."

Akira finds the spaces Ginger has in her psyche, the spaces she has wanted someone to fill. On the ride home, they sit close to each other. After two beers and an undetermined amount of sake, Ginger's head is dropping to one side. She fights to hold it upright, for if she doesn't fight it, her head will be on Akira's shoulder.

"Sleepy, Ginger?"

"A little. And a little drunk."

"You had a good time in Kyoto?"

"I had a very good time. But—I know this may sound neurotic—but do you worry much about earthquakes? I mean, I've read about them and about how devastating one would be in Tokyo during rush hour."

"I was in Kobe when the earthquake struck five years ago." His voice has changed volume, if not pitch.

"You were working there?"

"I went to judge a voice competition. The quake started early in the morning. I was still in bed."

"Were you frightened?" Our English teacher tries hard not to think of this man in his pajamas, and harder still of him *not* in them. She trusts the conductor is more in control of the train than she is in control of her thoughts.

"Sure. There was much loss of life. Roads and buildings crumbled. Too many fires to count."

"Was your wife worried about you? Or was she with you?"

"My wife was asleep at home in Osaka."

"I'm familiar with Kobe only from hearing about its beef."

"You'd like Kobe, Ginger. The Chinese character for it means *God's door*." He lowers his voice still more. "How do you know about my wife?"

"Sakiko mentioned her, that's all."

Sundown comes on the ride home, and their reflections in the window darken as twilight outstrips sunset. The train speeds along with a gentle rocking motion, and Ginger's body rises and falls as it does when she plays Brahms.

Sunday, July 9

What a lovely day it was for a teachers' outing—hot and humid, but that didn't affect our sightseeing. I wore a sunhat, and we found shade where we could. I'm tired, not sapped. Maybe my body is adjusting to this climate.

Hiro was waiting for me at the station when Akira and I returned. Sakiko is still out with Mai—Sakiko drove her, in their rusty hatchback, to a friend's house for studying. Sakiko is visiting with a friend of her own while waiting for Mai. Hiro and I have gone over what I'll do this week. I'll be discussing, with handpicked students, casual versus business English; giving cultural lessons to several classes; and holding a grammar question-and-answer session with staff. I'll have to give the cultural lessons some thought. We could practice shaking hands. I felt a number of limp handshakes at the post-assembly reception last week. Hiro told me the teachers want to know things like the difference between *persuade* and *convince*. As for business English, most business writers would do well to write more casually. If they'd rid their writing of four-syllable words like *intransigent* and *repopulate*, people might want to read what they write. I tried to explain this to Hiro, as a start; he said I was making no sense. That's because it's something people don't want to believe, that short words are better than long words. I don't mind taking an unpopular stand. I'll tell them what I believe, not what they want to hear.

Speaking of beliefs, Akira apologized after dinner for hitting me with a bunch of Schubert comments on the train to Kyoto this morning. He said he didn't mean to make me feel uncomfortable, figured I was Catholic, and wanted to get a Catholic's perspective on the matter. I hadn't taken it personally, although I thought it a bit odd how he went on about what may or may not have been Schubert's theology. It was as though Akira was testing me.

That said, to be perfectly honest, Mr. Sato is very appealing. I like the way he flatters me and the way he talks about literature. I've spent the last decade questioning my attractiveness; Akira lets me know I'm attractive. And shallow of me though it may be, I like the way he looks, all taut and dark and refined. But I need to gain control of myself. He's married, he's off limits, and even if he were to divorce he'd be off limits. The Church has taken great strides toward ecumenism, so I could marry a non-Catholic, but not a divorced man. I can't believe I'm writing this. A few hours with someone and I'm imagining myself marrying him!

I'm going to stop writing now. Sakiko had prepared my bath before she went out, and that plastic tub cover kept the water warm, so I'm showered and soaked and relaxed, or I was until I started to write. I've got to quit. I'm determined to get a good night's sleep.

Oh, I bought a new journal in Kyoto. At this rate I may have to buy yet another. Akira was interested in the fact that I'm keeping a journal. He asked if he would figure in it. I simply said I'm keeping a faithful account of what I'm doing on this trip. I didn't tell him how I'm feeling about writing (and I *couldn't* tell him how I'm feeling about him). I'd always thought writing was for someone else to do, someone more creative than I am. I don't know whether to castigate myself for being a hypocrite, asking my students to keep a journal when I haven't done it, or if I should congratulate myself for having given my students a chance to exercise their creativity.

One more thing—as we were walking out of the station, Akira said he wants to see me again. I said, "Sure, maybe I could meet your wife." He started to respond, but Hiro appeared alongside us all of a sudden, and Akira didn't finish his thought.

Monday, July 10

The school day started out well, and it isn't ending badly, but what was in the middle was ghastly. A toilet-paper-stuck-to-the-shoe affair.

Hiro took me to his first class, second-year English, handed me his book, and left me alone with his students. This was a surprise to me; it may have been a surprise to his students as well. The students stay in the same room all day, forty to a classroom—and to think *we* complain about class size. I don't see how the students get any individual attention, or how the teachers hold discussions. There are lockers in the rooms for the students, no hall lockers. The teachers move from room to room.

Hiro's students told me they're in the middle of Chapter Six, participles leading to gerunds leading to infinitives. They told me English is taught by the book—it sounded like page by measured page. The English is more technical material than is found in most American curricula. I asked what American or English literature they read, eliciting no response but for a boy who admitted to *Dilbert*, which made the other students laugh.

I asked if they had questions about English.

"Would you please tell us when to omit the sign of the infinitive?"

"When does one use *continual* and when *continuous*?"

"When is it correct to use *which* and when *that*?"

"What's the difference between Cajun speech and Creole dialect?"

I still don't know if they were posturing or if they actually wanted to know the answers. For questions I couldn't answer, I said I'd get back to them. I did that a lot. One question I *could* answer was, "Under what circumstances should I hyphenate a compound noun?" That's of course one of my specialties, although I'm afraid I lost some of them when I distinguished compounds formed of nouns of equal value and those formed with a modifying noun acting upon the dominant noun. Several students nodded their heads as I spoke, so I figured I was getting through; others wrote, but their bodies didn't reflect understanding. They held their pens poised after I finished each sentence, as though if I said one thing more, *then* they would get it. I went over the rule several times, adding new examples. I still don't think they understood.

I told Hiro's students if they continue to study English, their grammar skills will at least equal those of educated Americans, and that they should work extra hard on *speaking* English. Hiro uses textbook English when he speaks, and I understand him easily; still his English is shrouded with a robust Japanese accent. His students could use a native English speaker to model pronunciation on an ongoing basis.

I talked about the creative writing assignments I give my classes at Confederate. The students said no English teacher at their school assigns creative writing. I suggested they write a quatrain this week, and if they put it in my shoe cupboard, I'll give them comments in a couple days. I showed them my pocket rhyming dictionary, and we chewed up some time running through rhymes. I read them the —*oop* rhymes, including dupe, goop, poop, soup, and nincompoop. I expected laughter, at least a little, but they simply took notes.

Hiro arrived at the bell, out of breath. Before he and I left the class, the students still in their seats, and the Japanese literature teacher waiting in the hall for us to leave, Hiro asked me to demonstrate "some fine points of pronunciation." He said many Japanese don't hear the difference between *bat* and *but*, so he asked me to model forming one's mouth for those words, which I did, and then he asked me if he and his students could look into my mouth as I said the words. I thought he was joking, so I brushed off his remark and packed up my materials. Now I'm not sure he *was* joking. Just as I wonder how opera singers roll their baroque *r*'s, I suppose the Japanese wonder how English speakers make certain sounds. I hadn't thought until today how similar our short *a* and short *u* must sound to the Japanese. I looked in my mouth a few minutes ago to see what Hiro wanted to see.

After Hiro's class I was due in the principal's office to meet with the head of the English department and the PTA president. That's what the woman was introduced to me as—the PTA president. How did Japan get the

PTA? She looked like the dragon lady from a B movie—hair pulled back into a bun, high cheekbones, pencil-thin body, straight skirt, tailored blouse. She was so intense, it was as though she was holding a magnifying glass between the window and me, trying to burn a hole through me. She kept smacking the notebook on her lap and talking about how they have to keep their students at the top of the standardized tests curve. She spoke English beautifully, but with an annoying British accent (although that particular accent has never rubbed me the wrong way before). She spoke to the principal in Japanese at every opportunity, cutting me out of the conversation. She sounded strident. The principal responded to her in English. The department chairman hardly said a word.

We went over matters of curriculum, and they asked me if I'd review some textbooks and write up my recommendations for adoption, as well as evaluate course syllabi. I raised the issue of teaching English literature in addition to grammar. Madam President said she didn't want teachers to take class time for material that wouldn't be tested on college entrance exams. Ignorant of just what English appears on Japanese standardized tests, I couldn't exactly refute her point, but I did argue that time spent in reading literature, and in writing, is not time wasted. I know studying literature raises SAT scores, so I shared that with the group. What they do with my recommendations is up to them, not me.

I didn't lay eyes on Akira—why do I care about Akira?—until this afternoon, *mon après-midi horrible*. He was in the front office, alas, when I arrived in my blood-soaked clothes. I pretended he wasn't there. But let me back up. This morning I'd felt a bit gassy but hadn't thought much of it, figuring it was Sakiko's strong, European-style coffee not mixing entirely well with my digestive juices. I should have realized I was about to start my period, but it wasn't due for a few days. During my session with the principal I felt the cramps come on. I also started to feel a little wet between the legs, but I figured it had more to do with—oh, never mind.

What happened next is too embarrassing for words. I would never want anyone to read this, but my need to set it down is greater than my fear someone will see it. When the meeting in the principal's office ended, I stood and walked toward the door. I was wearing my light blue A-line skirt. Unbeknownst to me, the back of it had acquired a cranberry-colored circle the size of a small head of lettuce. Mrs. Kitajima—that's the PTA president—followed me out the principal's door, on my heels, and whispered in my ear, "We must get you to the clinic, Ginger-san." Intuitively I knew what had happened. Mrs. K. walked behind me, her hand on my shoulder, as we made our way through the outer office and toward the clinic. And I'd resented her commanding presence in the meeting! I was glad someone took pity on me and took charge. I can't remember what the chairs in the principal's office were upholstered with. I hope it was something that could be wiped clean. I can't bring myself to ask about them.

While I was cleaning up in the clinic lavatory, Mrs. K. called Sakiko and asked her to bring me a change of clothes. Sakiko didn't want to rummage through my things, so she brought me a dress she wore when she was pregnant with Mai. She had guessed, rightly, that I wouldn't fit into her clothes—non-maternity clothes, that is, and she had given away all her maternity things except for this one dress. Her mother had made it for her, and she said she can't part with it. She hopes Mai will wear it some day. I didn't want to say anything, but I highly doubt Mai will wear it. It's darling but looks very 1980s—a tent dress in a striped calico of tiny pink flowers. Sakiko thought the dress might not look quite right on me—she was right, it looked like a maternity dress—so she included a belt. The belt was too small. Sakiko's underwear did fit, though I worried all afternoon the elastic waistband would give out and they'd fall to the floor as I walked down the hall. They are basic white cotton briefs, like my mother used to wear. Sakiko had also brought a pair of her stockings, which I stuck in my bag.

By the time Sakiko arrived at the school with the clothes, my cramps had turned to tractor pulls. I was nauseated (not *nauseous*, unless I was making other people sick, a distinct possibility, given the circumstances). My codeine-improved Tylenol #3 was back at the Murakamis' house, but Mrs. Kitajima had a pain-killer in her pocketbook that was good and strong. It put me to sleep in the clinic until school was over. I haven't had bleeding this severe for years.

I would have liked to come back to the Murakamis' right after school. Hiro had a meeting, though—something about the baseball team—and he'd left a note for me with Yoko, the office worker who directed me to the music room last week. The note said we wouldn't be leaving school until six forty-five. I knew Sakiko and Mai had errands to run; besides, I couldn't have asked Sakiko to come pick me up after the trouble she took for me today. There was also a note from the art teacher. He'd heard, presumably from Hiro, that I had some time to kill (what else had he heard? about my bleeding? about my trip to Kyoto with Akira?) and invited me to the art studio after school. I went more out of curiosity than anything else. Teru Tanabe—that's the art teacher's name; he's in his early thirties, I'd guess—was delightful, making fun of himself at every turn, especially at his hacked-up English. He kept saying, "No flied lice, today, Missy, no flied lice," emitting a snorting laugh every time he said it. I couldn't help but laugh, once I was sure he was joking.

We made a monotype. I painted a Plexiglas plate with special printing inks. I chose my favorite colors: blue, green, and violet, analogous colors. As the paint—I painted lily-like flowers—was drying on the plate, we dampened a sheet of Japanese paper. It seemed delicate, yet it was strong enough to take the rubbing we did when we laid it over the dried paint. Between the image on the paper and the paper's dimensions—tall and narrow—the print turned out looking Japanese. Teru put the print to dry between sheets of newsprint, laying old vinyl record albums over the newsprint to weight it, so the print will dry flat. He told me to come by the art room tomorrow to pick it up. There was a nice ghost image of the flowers left on the Plexi, which Teru said he almost hated to wash off.

While I was painting, Akira stopped by to offer me a ride home. I was glad I was wearing a full-length painting smock, both to protect Sakiko's dress and to hide it. (The dress is a mini on me, the smock itself not particularly long.) I had to decline his offer—not only was I in the middle of painting, but Hiro was expecting to see me at six forty-five.

On the ride home Hiro and I came upon a Japanese hearse. I thought I was hallucinating when a gilded, boxy-topped, black Lincoln Continental rolled by. The top was like a shrine, even fancier and more ornamented than Bernini's papal altar. A gold dragon lay atop the hearse. Hiro said the hearse was Shinto because of the dragon. A Buddhist hearse wouldn't sport a dragon, but possibly lotus leaves. What I'd give to see a hearse like that go by in Nether Gorge!

Tonight for dinner Sakiko fixed *okonomiyaki*—Japanese pancakes. They reminded me of the zucchini rounds Steve and I used to make with the harvest of our little summer garden.

Sakiko has washed my clothes. She got the blood out. My skirt and underpants are hanging in the garden. Hiro is out there now, smoking.

Tuesday, July 11

Faculty parties must be the same everywhere: uneasy spouses, inebriated teachers, too-friendly men, the woman of the house in need of roller skates. Tonight's was like all the others and different, too—piles of shoes inside the door, no handshaking, no hugging, no air kissing, no open-mouthed roars of laughter from women.

The party was on a farm in the country, hosted by a science teacher and his wife, Mr. and Mrs. Fujita. Their given names zoomed right past me and out onto the evening breezes. They live on the farm with Mr. F.'s parents. The parents work the farm, as does the teacher's wife—unwillingly, Sakiko told me. On our drive out there, the sinking sun cast long shadows on the hills and trees—cedars, maples, pines—then, as we neared the house, sculpted trees drifted into sight and welcomed us up the long driveway. A mammoth umbrella tree covers a large swatch of property behind the house. The Fujitas had set up tables and chairs under it, but we spent a lot of time inside too.

The house itself is low-slung and airy, many windows opening onto pastoral views. Floors in honeyed wood, walls in cream, Danish modern furniture, built-in bookshelves in cherry lining the walls—it all looked very scholarly and dig-into-able. The younger Mrs. F. is a journalist in what little time she has—she writes a gardening column for an Osaka newspaper. The teacher and his wife have two children who are away at school, so there's lots of room with only the four adults there. The house reminded me of lodges I've seen written up in the writers' magazines that I flip through in the library, places you can go to get away from it all and finish a manuscript. I would like to be staying in the Fujitas' house, although that thought makes me feel disloyal to Hiro and Sakiko, who have been so kind.

The house changed character as it filled with people. What had seemed a building of repose and calm soon was full of commotion, as everyday colleagues said to each other, I'm sure, the same thing they say every day. As far as I knew I was the only person new to that wide and noisy circle. The mid-week party was unusual, given that school's still in session, but a group of the social studies teachers is leaving before week's end for a conference in Nagoya. Tonight was their last chance to be together before summer vacation, what there is of it. I was glad to be feeling better—after yesterday's attack of cramps, things have only improved for my poor belly.

My sushi dreams came to a consummation tonight at the party. So much for pinwheels and Barbecups— the Fujitas had party platters of *nigiri* and *maki* sushi that made my head spin. I tried one piece of everything and two or three of my favorites, losing track after many glorious moments of gluttony. (This diary writing does make one conscious of one's sin, after it's too late to do anything about it.) There was sashimi too, lovely slices of tuna and yellowtail, also a chopped fish mixed with sour and salty pickled plums. It was delicious, and I had two or three helpings of it, then asked Sakiko what it was. She grinned, and in high spirits she let me know exactly what I'd eaten: raw chicken.

My appetite returned in time for the *mikan* served in a giant copper bowl, the orange of the fruit reflecting off the metallic container, the whole thing glowing like a pot of fire. The bowl sat on a mahogany dining table polished to a high sheen, as if it were set up for a Dutch still life. The elder Fujitas are very dignified and spoke at length with me about their travels—they've been to Spain, China, Uruguay. They struck me as managerial rather than agricultural. On the way home Sakiko confirmed my suspicions: they *run* the farm rather than farm it themselves. Their daughter-in-law handles their accounts and correspondence.

In the Fujitas' library I sat on an antique oak chair with a cane seat. It reminded me of the chairs I used when I was a child, the ones in the Lockton public library. The chairs were ordinary and utilitarian back then, but now they're charming, much in demand. I used to sit in the main reading room, the light from a banker's lamp shining squarely onto the middle of my table, the table's aging varnish having turned its surface a dark, nutty brown. The smell of books was all around me, the room's hush something I thought could never be breached. (And now in libraries people talk in ordinary, outside voices.)

I used to stick my fingers into the holes of a chair as I read, picturing myself as the boy holding back the waters from the lowlands, stemming the tide as it worked, back and forth, back and forth, to penetrate the dike. I would be in a trance, between my reading and my ever-present fantasies, losing track of my fingers, losing sensation in them, until one day when I poked a finger in far enough and firmly enough that it got stuck and turned blue. No one was near me and my preadolescent self in the reading room that day, but instead of calling out and violating the quiet of the library, I squat-walked the chair all the way to the front of the building, to the circulation desk, the chair stuck to my finger, my finger to the chair, the sharp edge of dried palm making a bloody gash at the base of my middle finger. A little Vaseline applied by the assistant librarian helped ease my finger out, my embarrassment lasting much longer than it took the cut to heal. I could tell the librarians were pointing me out to each other for months after that when I walked in the door. My shame almost made me want to abandon my borrowing privileges.

A cane chair brings to mind other things too. For example, I can't see a cane chair without thinking of the work of Juan Gris and Pablo Picasso. Gris, Picasso, Georges Braque, all exploring their cubist territory—how exciting it must have been to live their lives, to spend their days! I wish I could step back in time and live through this last century, to see the changes as they were happening, changes of science, medicine, warfare, production, the arts. Are our ancestors shadows in our lives now, or were we shadows in their lives then? In Braque's work sometimes the shadow seems more important than the shape itself, which makes me wonder if Braque was thinking, as he worked, about the shadows we leave around us as we pass through life.

I should mention my conversation this evening with several of the school's English teachers. They asked me what my pet peeves of language are—what a question! No one has ever asked me that—either because no one wants to know, or because I'm always telling people about these thorns in my side *sua sponte*. It was thrilling to think someone wanted a harangue on the destruction of the English language. I gave them an earful. I offered *veggies* as the prime example of where we're headed, that hated word—it's a usurper of, a pretender to, a perfectly good word of three or four syllables—depending on how your parents pronounced it—with its Latin roots related to *vitality* and to words like *vigor, excitement*, and *arousal*. I know this appears to contradict what I said yesterday about how business writers should ban four-syllable words from their vocabs. I mean *vocabularies*. But appearances deceive; I'm not contradicting myself. There's just no connection between a word like *vegetable* and one like *implementation* (even worse than yesterday's examples—five syllables) other than they both have Latin roots. Moreover, the point isn't whether to use the word *vegetable* at all but whether to truncate it to an infantile-sounding substitute. Can't we keep anything as it has been? Is every word open to reinvention? The thought of millions of American parents saying to their high-chaired kids, "Now, darling, it's time to eat your veggies, okay?" makes me sick. (Parents asking their children if discipline is okay with them, as in "I'm going to put you in 'time out' now, little Johnny, okay?" also drives me nuts, but it would have been a stretch for me to start down that path this evening.)

I went on like this for quite a while, the teachers nodding intently, although I think they were just being polite. I don't believe they followed a thing I said. That didn't matter to me, for soon I got going with my preposition irritation, explaining that American verbs now come entailed with a preposition that adds no value. Plumbers say they'll change *out* the fixtures; what happened to plain old *change the fixtures?* Or what people do after a work*out* at the gym—they shower *up*. That's what I hear phys ed teachers say to their classes—"Okay, time to shower up!" But I suppose if you hose something *down*, you might as well shower *up*.

Speaking of hosing down reminded me of one of Reggie's habits that tickled my growing audience when I related it to them. (I hope I wasn't betraying Reggie, either this evening or on Sunday when I told Akira about her fan-in-the-bangs problem. We were laughing at her, which isn't polite, but some of her more eccentric habits are already known far beyond the family.) Reggie thinks the groceries from our local supermarket are so dirty—the boxes, bags, and jugs they come in, that is—that she hoses them off in the kitchen sink when she brings them in from the store. She doesn't do cans, of course, as the paper wrappers would be a mess; nor does she wash off cartons of ice cream, for fear of meltdown, but frozen vegetables (a quick wash), half-gallons of milk, packages of cheese—the first stop for all of it is her sink. This is a systematic improvement from the first few times she took to washing her groceries, when she dumped the contents of her bags on her lawn as soon as she got home and used her garden hose and a squirt bottle of watered-down bubble bath on the whole caboodle. She soon saw that this was a scattershot approach and that the situation called for refinement, like soaking her grapes in hot, soapy water to kill the germs. Hence the more limited approach in the sink. Everyone laughed at the story, then one of the women had to break the spell; she asked if I'm like Reggie. I was diplomatic. I said my sister is a much nicer person than I am. When I said it, it was more or less a flippant response, just to bring an end to the conversation. As I think of it, though, I think it was one of those comments that, as a spontaneous, unconscious remark, reveals something about the truth.

At the party I was surrounded by people hungry to hear my impressions of their country. I flattered them, saying everything's been wonderful, for what's to be gained by crabbing about the heat? Indeed, the heat's been my only complaint, although some of that I bring on myself. Case in point: the Fujitas were serving a fabulous punch, which I thought would be cooling me off (they didn't have the air conditioning on), although I did surmise there was a *sukoshi* of alcohol in it. (My vocabulary is increasing rapidly!) By the time I realized how much *shochu* I'd drunk (the ride home was very instructional— *shochu* is a flavorless drink, like vodka in that way, and tonight was served in the fruit punch), and how hot and sweaty I was, there wasn't much I could do but enjoy it. Fujita the Younger put on pop music—a little Elton John, some early Beatles, Billy Joel, Carole King—and then the assistant principal came over and asked me if I'd lead a conga line. By that time I didn't care what I did. I got us started, and we wended our way through the house and garden, with a slight hiccup at the front door as people collected their shoes for the outdoor portion of our dance. Hiro was immediately behind me, his hands on my hips, encouraging me to lead us into the koi pool. So everyone kicked off their shoes again, the men rolling up their pant legs, for the plunge. I haven't laughed so hard in years.

Where was I? Oh, yes—people were drinking heavily, and it wouldn't put too fine a point on it to say many of the men were flat-out drunk. Hiro's face was red from one can after another of those tall Sapporos. As I sat on my regained cane chair, recovering from rockin' round the clock, hoping for a little quiet, a little time to *observe* rather than to *be part of* the action, a man—the boyfriend, apparently, of one of the few women teachers—sidled up next to me, scraping his own chair across the polished floor as he scooted over from his little conversation group. Upon reaching me he lurched to his feet, and the next thing I knew, in full sight of everyone, he'd taken up a position behind my chair and had begun running his arms along my neck and shoulders, then up and down my arms! As I was picking his limbs up and depositing them back into his territory, he fell forward onto me, and only the back of my chair kept his weight from knocking me onto the floor. And I'd thought Japan would be different from Nether Gorge!

Sakiko appeared at my side just then, with her friend Mama Mia or something like that. Mama Mia has one of those husky voices that seem to be low, but, when used as a musical instrument, will shockingly reach Queen of the Night highs. (Her voice reminded me of the voice of that uppity woman who worked with Steve.) Anyway, Mama had the nerve to say to me, "You look like affair, Ginger-san." Well, I stood up in a rush, leaving Lover-san to catch himself from sliding in his striped socks to the floor. I said, "I beg your pardon, but I am wholly innocent of any wrongdoing." To which Mama Mia replied, archly it seemed to me, "It too bad Akira-san not here at party. Wife need him home this evening. You should meet Megumi-san some time—she so sweet." Sakiko giggled, and I had to ask myself where her allegiance lies.

Now it all seems quite harmless, but I admit I immediately took umbrage at Mama's statement. In the face of her remark, I started to pull myself up tall so I could look down my nose at her, intending to say in the most serene of voices, "Excuse me, I am above reproach." The trouble was I literally choked on my words, saliva having pooled at the back of my mouth as I'd concentrated on standing up. I had to clear my throat several times, and by the time I was on my feet I'd entirely forgotten where I was going with my rejoinder. "Excuse me while I investigate the powder room" is what came out of my mouth, and I turned on my heel, leaving Sakiko and her friend trading glances with each other, as if they knew something I didn't.

SEVEN

Gari

For ten days now Ginger has recorded her thoughts, her words, and her deeds, and has accomplished all this in her old-fashioned diary, supplemented by electronically encoded messages sent from Hiro's computer and by paper letters and cards to family and friends. After years of writing only the occasional academic paper and informal correspondence, Ginger has found in her fingers a new outlet. That her usual circle of friends and telephone connections are unavailable galvanizes her need to communicate (mostly with herself) through ramped-up means. Learning a new expertise, and an introspective one at that, Ginger finds herself thinking more deeply about what is important to her. But this business of Ginger's interior life is a matter for a more leisurely moment, when she isn't playing a dangerous game.

Notwithstanding her avowal that her relationship with Akira is and must remain a professional relationship, her new-found delight in her pen has caused Ginger to spend two hours writing three lines to thank Akira for her trip to Kyoto. (She has also thanked the principal for Saturday night's dinner, the letter written on classic ivory stock, for which Sakiko made a special trip to the stationery store.) Ginger wants Akira to know how much she enjoyed the day, end of story. Ginger has checked and rechecked the neutral-in-tone, *pro forma* missive for unintended innuendos. She has combed its diction, careful to use only the King's English. She has had to place her trust in an online dictionary, for Ginger's copy of *Webster's New International Dictionary, Second Edition* (not the third, more liberal edition) is safe and sound on its own inclined, revolving stand in her Nether Gorge home. People like Ginger sometimes want to freeze-dry the language at a certain point in time. They fail to keep in mind that the English language is a living, growing organism, not an insect caught in amber. They often don't accept forward motion for themselves or for the world around them.

Why Ginger doesn't put the note in Akira's mail slot in the school office is a question only she can answer. If you were to ask her, while she's strolling down that music room hallway with a little nervousness in her gut, she would regale you with a host of rationalizations: she's embarrassed to enter the office after Monday's fiasco; she has never seen Akira in the teacher's room and doesn't know which desk is his; she has no idea which shoe cupboard is his and so can't put the note there; she doesn't want to trouble Hiro—he does so much for her already—by asking him to give it to Akira; she wouldn't dream of mailing the note to Akira's home. When a person has his mind set on something, can anyone sway him?

Within the acoustics of that hall, Ginger hears the piano beneath a soprano's muffled voice. The keyboard's sound is susurrous, whispering; someone is applying the damper pedal as lightly as a leaf floats to the ground. The door to the room is closed, and Ginger stops shy of its narrow vertical window. Closing her eyes to concentrate, she picks up the harmony's stepwise motion, technically expressed by rising bass notes, first two whole steps, then a half. The notes turn up as counterpoint in the next phrase's melody, but in that phrase the related motion is first a half-step, then two whole steps.

These are scientific matters, a gloss on the intuitive response a person of Ginger's age and background has for this particular song. For despite her learned scrutiny, our traveler's recognition of the tune is subconscious: "Londonderry Air," "Danny Boy." The song is formulaic even in Japan, but as jaded as Ginger is to clichés, this one touches her. She feels silly that it touches her, thinking it shouldn't, but she can't help it. That her father's name was Daniel gives her an excuse, which she uses when someone catches her tearing up over the song. She would find her eyes wet now if she weren't so surprised to hear the song in this place, for she wasn't aware that it's a popular song in Japan.

The words are hard to make out, but Ginger guesses they are not a mother's words foretelling that her son will pray at her grave. Ginger looks through the glass and sees a boy sitting at the piano and a girl standing with her back to the door. She sees also, not surprisingly, the music teacher. She studies his profile—the India-ink ponytail brushing his white collar, his eyebrow raised, his mouth open wide. The song is his now, and he repeats from among the lines the girl just sang: *Yea, would to God I were among the roses / That lean to kiss you as you float between.*

The music stops. Some seconds pass, and Akira throws the door wide open.

"Ginger!"

"I didn't mean to interrupt. You've a lesson in progress."

"A performer always wants an audience. Please." Akira motions for his caller to enter.

Ginger steps across the threshold and greets the students. The boy rises; both the girl and the boy bow to her. Akira gets a chair from the back of the room and seats Ginger in the front row, the only row, of his audience.

"Yoshi? Reiko?"

Yoshi sits back down. Through blindingly smudged glasses, he plays the introductory measures, and Reiko begins to sing.

Would God I were the tender apple blossom
That floats and falls from off the twisted bough,
To lie and faint within your silken bosom,
Within your silken bosom, as that does now!

The pianist continues with his rising bass notes, but Reiko has stopped.

"*Sumimasen.*"

"Practice your English while Mrs. O'Neill is with us."

Reiko drops her eyes to her music stand. "I feel—I feel this song is for man to sing. It is man's song to woman." A brown plastic band holds Reiko's hair back from her face, signaling her widow's peak.

Akira lets out a small groan. "Have I made a bad choice with this song?"

Ginger speaks up. "You make a good point, Reiko. This song's lyrics make more sense coming from a man. Maybe Mr. Sato will sing it for us."

Reiko smiles and moves to the side of the room.

"I'd be more than happy to sing," Akira says, a cock in the barnyard. Critic and performer exist in a symbiotic, codependent relationship. Akira nods to Yoshi, and this time the boy inclines closer to the keys, hands and feet a bit heavier than before. Akira's voice fills the room with the softness of a spring morning.

Would God I were the tender apple blossom
That floats and falls from off the twisted bough,
To lie and faint within your silken bosom,
Within your silken bosom, as that does now!
Or would I were a little burnished apple
For you to pluck me, gliding by so cold,
While sun and shade your robe of lawn will dapple,
Your robe of lawn and your hair's spun gold.

Yea, would to God I were among the roses
That lean to kiss you as you float between,
While on the lowest branch a bud uncloses,
A bud uncloses to touch you Queen.
Nay, since you will not love, would I were growing
A happy daisy in the garden path;
That so your silver foot might press me going,
Might press me going even unto death!

One might have thought a Japanese man singing these familiar and beloved verses from the island of Ireland would come close to the incongruity of the Rolling Stones singing "A Mighty Fortress is Our God." Akira manages to transcend that bias, though, leaving Ginger with a slightly giddy head. Akira's mild modulations, like a calm sea breaking onto shore, portray a man in a sunlit garden wooing his lady fair. However, when Akira comes to the line, *A happy daisy in the garden path*, the transcendence ends for Ginger, for it's at that point she recalls her Sunday *faux pas* on the path of the Peaceful Dragon, as well as many other details of that day.

The room is nearly silent, the only movement that of harmonic vibration evaporating into damp air.

"So you like it then, my singing, Ginger O'Neill?"

Ginger pulls herself together to address that which the school setting calls for. "If Reiko wants to sing this song, she might try the 'Danny Boy' lyrics, if her voice can carry the weight of a mother's love. Some young singers perform it without conviction, making it a charade of a mother's bidding farewell to her child. The singer must work in her mind to imagine having a child, and then imagine saying good-bye to that child."

"Do you think a person outside a particular tradition can interpret that culture's feelings through music, Ginger? With sensitivity, I mean?"

Reiko and Yoshi are quiet, paging through music.

"You've got to be careful," says Ginger. "Plácido Domingo is not exactly persuasive when he sings 'Danny Boy,' and it doesn't matter whether he's supposed to be Danny's mother or Danny's father. His pronunciation of words like *dead* and *tread*, combined with his labored phrasing, distract the listener from his expression." Ginger is warming to her impromptu critic's role, calling up years of reading liner notes and watching music videos. "On the other hand, Yehudi Menuhin was a Jewish violinist who truly carried the spirit of Bach's St. Matthew Passion."

"True, but *Erbarme dich* refers not to Christ but to God."

Ginger may be in over her head, yet she is undaunted. "I saw a video of Menuhin in his concert with the Pope. It was an otherwise messy performance that included a chamber orchestra and a contralto, but I wanted Menuhin to play that *obbligato* for me, those same few notes, over and over, into eternity. When I'm dying, that's what I want to hear." Ginger rises, takes a few steps toward the door, then stops and turns back to Akira. "Are you familiar with Ben Onslow's recording of 'Danny Boy' with the Denver Philharmonic?"

Akira shakes his head.

"Strings only," Ginger says, "arrangement by Percy Grainger. No vocals. It's the most beautiful music I've ever heard." She is at no loss for favorites, for hyperbole. Indeed, Ginger's had a crush on Ben Onslow since she heard him conduct that same piece of music on a Christmas trip she took with Bernie and Reggie. He looked like a spliced-together Mickey Mouse and Donald Duck, summoning up music with his arms as Mickey did in *The Sorcerer's Apprentice*, coaxing sound from the sea. The effect was especially witty because he was wearing a white jacket and black trousers and looking something like a bird-man. Ginger tried to get backstage after the performance but was turned away by ushers who guarded the inner sanctum. She'd wanted Onslow to autograph her program.

"Maybe I can find that recording," Akira says.

"The imagination, through music, can tell a story much better than words can, don't you think?"

Akira nods. "That is what music is for."

Ginger again moves toward the door.

"Where are you going?"

"I thought you'd want to finish your lesson with your students."

"Don't leave now." He summons her back with squiggles of his hand. "Takemitsu Toru, who composed the score for the movie *Ran*, wrote a transcription of 'Londonderry Air' for guitar. Do you know it?"

"I don't."

Akira scratches his forehead. "Takemitsu was able to cross cultural boundaries with his guitar music, but I worry about my students working on Christian music without knowing much about Christianity."

"It has to be hardest with vocal music," Ginger says. "For me the accent, more than any supposed faith, is tough to get past. Other listeners, especially those who don't know the language the singer is using, might not have that—"

"People tell me I resemble Maestro Nagano."

Ginger smiles. "Well, I've been told I look like Renée Fleming. Or Sally Field."

"Excuse me, *Sensei*," Reiko says, picking up her satchel and stuffing it with files, "but I must go to next class." She bows and is gone.

"I can work with Reiko later on her pronunciation," Ginger says.

Yoshi is studying a stack of music on his lap. Akira speaks to him in Japanese, and the boy finds two pages of music and plays the opening measures of a Chopin waltz in A minor. It's a posthumous composition. Ginger has practiced this song herself, trying to achieve a consistently brisk tempo and never quite succeeding. Yoshi's fingers are defter than Ginger's.

"Ginger," Akira says, his voice slow and deliberate, "I would like to dance with you." Yoshi's head is bent over the piano.

"Do you think that's wise?"

"Don't you like to dance?" Akira slides his arm around the waistband of Ginger's skirt, giving Ginger a breathless feeling, as if a sushi chef had hidden an extra spot of wasabi in her *nigiri-zushi*. Akira takes her right hand in his left. She rests her left forearm on his shirt, settling her hand on his collar. She needn't stretch her arms or stand on her toes. Akira is a mirror image of Ginger, but muscular where she is yielding—arms, back, and legs.

Yoshi commingles the first two quarter-note chords in each bar by means of the damper pedal. Right before the third beat, he lifts his foot, so the dancers experience a lightness, an effervescence, to the final beat of the measure. In their bodies is a *luft*, that same breath as in Yoshi's pedal work. Yoshi uses his youthful energy, pressing and releasing, pressing and releasing. When he presses down, he does so deeply, his hips and torso following the movement of his leg and foot. Yoshi plays the waltz *rubato*, robbing some notes of their duration to fit in more time for others. The ambiguities could make for dancing trouble, but Akira leads his partner without hesitation.

As far as Ginger's concerned, she could be in a Viennese ballroom, a spy during World War II. She could be circling the worn hardwood floor in the arms of a Japanese diplomat, chandeliers establishing blurry shadows of her viridian moiré gown as she and her partner live in a world of their own making. Ginger is held close, tucked in, yin alongside her partner's yang.

"How are you feeling after Sunday's sake? Sometimes our national drink delivers more than one expects." Akira looks directly at Ginger, their faces so close that his breath is upon her, his mouth about to graze hers.

"I could have stopped with one glass." She moves her hand up and under his pony tail, touching the base of his neck with her index finger.

Akira's laugh falls warmly on Ginger's skin. "You have an American expression about being 'pickled' when you've drunk too much, no? I will think of you as *gari*. Pickled Ginger, with skin as translucent as the finest gari."

"Translucent?" Ginger enjoys eating pickled ginger with her sushi, but she has never analyzed its ability to allow light to pass through it.

"Your complexion is like the sheerest, best gari."

"What is just plain *ginger* in Japanese?" To her credit, Ginger is keeping up a line of earnest conversation.

"*Shoga*." Akira pauses for a moment, then releases Ginger from the dance position. He takes her face in his hands. "It's as though when you were born, the gods dipped the tips of their fingers in strawberry juice and gave your skin a gentle rubbing. You are pink." He takes her in his arms again and resumes the dance.

Ginger is silent, wondering what the right thing to say is, what the right thing to do is. How should she behave in these circumstances? Meanwhile, Ginger is having physical sensations that she had with Ken at the reservoir, and with her husband.

"I'd hoped to see you and your wife last night."

"At the faculty party? I never go to those!"

"Sakiko's friend mentioned your wife to me."

"This school is full of gossipers."

"I was embarrassed."

"There's nothing to be embarrassed about. I told my wife I was taking our partnership ambassador on a sightseeing excursion. That was the truth. I have no control over what my wife did with that information."

"Still, I'm uncomfortable about it."

"Look, Ginger, I have an idea. Let me talk to you again before you leave today."

"I don't know."

"Will you meet me in the north hallway at six-fifteen?"

"If Hiro and I haven't gone home by then."

Yoshi has quit playing, gathered his things, and left the room. Akira leads Ginger by the hand to the piano. She is unsteady, possibly from the twirling.

"Sit next to me. I have something for you." Akira guides Ginger to the treble end of the bench, claiming the bass for himself. His fingers are long, elegant. Playing the initial measures of Schubert's "Serenade," his right arm skims the front of Ginger's dress as he reaches for the high notes. She doesn't lean back to avoid his touch. Akira's voice, that warm baritone, is at first a whisper. Ultimately, his power swells.

Lo, my song through the night
Pleads, my darling, with you;
Down in the quiet glen,
Sweetheart, come to me!

Treetops stirring,
Slender branches,
In the moon's light,
In the moon's light.
There will be no betrayers,
In the moon's light,
In the moon's light.

Do you hear the nightingales' rhythm?
Hush! they call to you,

With their notes so sweet and moving,
Urging you to me.

They know my only longing,
They know my grief,
They know my grief.
Gentle hearts are melted by their
Silvery tones at dark,
Silvery tones at dark.

Let your soul, your core, give way,
Darling, hear my prayer!
Quiv'ring, I await your answer!
Come, honor me! Yes, honor me!

EIGHT

Sashimi

The dragon is a whip of fire, lit from within, eyes glowing, scales iridescent. The sun sets behind him, in the West, over lands governed by other masters and other gods. In the dragon's land, the rhythm of the day, sharp and quick, is exchanged yen by yen for a slower beat, a deep-rooted beat, one that penetrates small spaces visible only by night's glow. These are the spaces among and between people's outward actions, these the openings in their hearts.

In lower Honshu, across Kansai, in and around the great city of Osaka (once called *Naniwa*, when it was the nation's capital), near the geographical center of Japan, in the area known as the Nation's Kitchen—for its role in satisfying the dragon's hunger—farmers weed fields until the soil beneath them disappears into the darkness. Widows take cemetery walks, paying respects to husbands

157

who, when alive, their wives couldn't imagine missing. Salarymen who aren't fortunate enough to be on holiday are tied up in meetings, meetings, meetings, their wives at home preparing dinner for the children the men hardly see. They look forward to little, these men do, finding pleasure in simple things like planning the evening's activities, even though such activities are largely a reproduction of last night's, hours spent with other salarymen in coarse bars. Illicit lovers find each other under a cover of darkness.

Dotonbori, in Namba, is Osaka's famous entertainment district, paper lanterns and neon lights blushing its features, fish restaurants crawling alongside its man-made waterway. Here our itinerant teacher, led with quick step by her distaff host, looks around herself with the wonder of a child, never having seen anything so captivating as this combination of electricity and imagination. It beats Times Square decisively, Dotonbori's conspiracy of canal and bridges its trump card.

Inside one of those fish restaurants, Ginger's and Sakiko's cold reflections ghost by the windows as they're shown to their table. The women remove their shoes and step up into a booth. The lights are soft pinpoints held in frosted glass teardrops that hang from the ceiling; the walls have been painted calla green. Incandescent bulbs set in soffits throw curved shadows over the ceiling.

Against the glow of the walls, Sakiko looks happy and young, the way a college student waiting for her date might look. The shiny surface of the table is a transparent acrylic poured over natural beach pebbles, and atop the table, like sailboats with broken masts, rest paper napkins and wrapped chopsticks. Ginger runs her hand over the table to touch its coolness, its slickness. Above the booth a print of a half-mad kabuki actor floats on a mat inside a burled wood frame. The outline of his mouth resembles a whale, the mammal's tail sticking up on the right, its head diving down on the left.

"I wish I had time to see a play," Ginger says, continuing the discussion they'd begun in the street, "but it will have to wait until my next visit to Japan. I want to see kabuki."

"We will go to kabuki next time."

"Will you come to visit us in the States?"

"I love to see White House. Ginger, will you order beer, or maybe sake?" The women wipe their hands with the hot, moist towels the waitress has served them.

"I think I've had enough alcohol lately. Hot tea is fine."

"You like sashimi, Ginger?"

"Usually. I don't want any more chicken sashimi, though."

"This is fish restaurant. No chicken here."

"Good. You know, I like sashimi, but a little goes a long way. The rice in sushi tempers the fishy taste and texture." Ginger looks across the room and then back at Sakiko. "I admire the grains of rice in *nigiri-zushi*, all of them lying in the same direction. It's so orderly. They are notes on a staff."

Sakiko stares at her friend. Ginger's imagination may move in ways Sakiko's doesn't. After a moment Sakiko says, "Sashimi comes with bowl of rice. Anyway, did you notice fish pool in big room?"

"I did." The women had walked past water swishing along in blue plastic channels. "Do we catch our own dinner?" Ginger jokes.

"Not exactly," Sakiko says, with no hint of comedy. "We tell staff what to catch for us. How does that sound?"

"Okay. I'll eat anything." After all, it's no worse than having the seafood clerk at the grocery store steam a lobster. Except that here, no one is going to cook the food.

Sakiko motions to the waitress. They speak in Japanese, the waitress nodding and pushing a throaty sound out through her closed lips. She slides away like a creek, sinuous in her long straight skirt and slippers.

"Sakiko, I want to ask your opinion."

"I can help you?"

"It seems I've got myself in a bit of a pickle." Ginger can't help but think of her last conversation with Akira.

"Pickle? What you mean, pickle?"

"Trouble."

Sakiko's eyes widen. "Oh?"

"Well, I'm not sure it's trouble, that's what I want your opinion about. Maybe it's nothing."

"It is about Akira-san?"

"How did you know?"

"People are same everywhere."

Ginger picks up her tea, burning her fingers on the handleless mug. "Akira has asked me to go to Awaji Island with him, to see the earthquake museum. The museum is built on the fault line. It will be an overnight trip, Saturday night."

Sakiko looks up from tracing figures on the table with her fingers. "Impossible!"

"What?"

"No one in a school—private school—has affair. Not with someone at school. Maybe think of it. Not do it. Only on TV drama."

"Sakiko, this is not an affair. Akira is on the committee. He said he has two rooms booked for us."

Sakiko shakes her head. "You fall in love with him, Ginger."

"Anyway, not that it applies to me, but Confederate teachers—"

"At your school? What they do?"

"Oh, nothing. It's not important." Ginger thinks better of telling Sakiko about the occasional intramural extramarital affair. It could jeopardize the partnership.

"Teacher at your school have affair? With each other?"

"I wouldn't say it's *impossible*."

"At our school, this never happen."

"Good. I told Akira I would go with him. I'd like to see more of your country."

"You like to see more of Akira-san. Natural. What do you think of ponytail?"

"Sakiko, to be honest, I find Akira, and his ponytail, very attractive."

"Nothing is wrong with looking." Sakiko is poker-faced. "He is rebel at school. Men teachers are supposed to have hair cut short."

The waitress serves miso soup.

"Where will you stay?"

"In a *ryokan*. I suppose you've stayed at a ryokan many times."

"I have never been to ryokan since I married," Sakiko says.

"I figured Japanese people went to ryokans all the time. Akira said I should experience one. In America we have nothing like them."

"You are lucky, Ginger. Traditional Japanese inn is special experience."

"Sakiko, I don't want to put you in the middle of this. I don't want to make it difficult for you to be both my host and part of your school's community."

"Not hard to do both."

"I don't know where to turn. I haven't been attracted like this to a man since my husband died."

"You are hungry for man."

"I've dated, but I've never felt much for the men I was dating."

"This is different?"

"It's silly, I know, but I can't stop thinking about Akira."

Sakiko nods. "Not silly."

"You'd never do anything like this, would you, Sakiko?"

"Ginger, I have husband. You don't." Sakiko fails to mention Akira's own marital status, but in Japan, as elsewhere, standards for the sexes can be quite different.

Before Ginger can respond, a young couple and their two children stop at the women's table. Sakiko introduces them to Ginger as neighbors and Ginger to them as a visiting English teacher from America. The husband speaks to Ginger in English; initially his wife listens, not speaking. When the children grow restless and run off, their mother follows them. The man keeps talking to Ginger. Sakiko rifles through her handbag, sips her tea, grazes Ginger's legs with her toes as she crosses and recrosses her legs.

"*Sensei*, how long did you say you'll be in Osaka?"

"Only ten more days."

"I am personnel manager. You can speak to my company about America. My employees want to improve English skills."

"My time is spoken for on this trip."

"You don't get time off?"

The waitress is waiting to set their sashimi order on the table. Sakiko speaks up, "Ginger-san wants to come back to Japan. She will stay with my husband and me again."

"Yes, that's a good idea," Ginger says, handing the man her business card. "Please get in touch with me if you can use me another summer."

The man accepts Ginger's card with both hands and examines it, then turns it over and looks at the back of it, which is blank. He removes his wallet from his breast pocket, inserting Ginger's card into a plastic sleeve and back into his wallet and pocket.

"It was nice to meet you, *Sensei. Ja mata.*"

"He was very bold," Sakiko comments, as she adjusts the location of the plates the waitress left.

"Don't you think it's odd he didn't give me one of his cards?"

"Maybe he didn't have card with him."

The sashimi platter holds gleaming slices of fish flesh, lined up like segments of a snake. The head of the freshly deceased *hamachi* stands next to the array, a watchful eye on his banquet.

"Please, Ginger. Eat."

Ginger bathes both sides of a piece of fish in soy sauce, opens her already-watering mouth, and rests the salty mixture on her tongue.

"How you like it, Ginger?"

Nodding her pleasure, Ginger happens to glimpse the fish's head on the platter, this time not dispassionately. The fish surely has moved.

"That fish is twitching at me, Sakiko. Its gills are quivering."

"Fresh! A moment ago alive, maybe in a way it still is. My husband, he likes to eat octopus still moving."

"Who is moving?"

"Octopus."

Ginger is steadfast. She will not lose her appetite. She will continue to eat. She just won't look at the fish's head.

"I'm thinking your school would be horrified to learn of my trip to Awaji, Sakiko, regardless what the room arrangements are. In spite of what I've just told your neighbor, maybe this will be my last trip."

"No, Ginger, you are natural traveler."

"Possibly, but I'm afraid I'm going to put the partnership at risk, as well as my morals. Not to mention Akira's marriage."

"You are not responsible for marriage of Akira-san."

"No?"

"Ginger, he is adult man. He is responsible for self. You are responsible for you."

"But it's not right. You said people in your school don't have affairs. There must be a reason."

"Sure. It makes mess for people around. This is different. You don't live here."

Sakiko seems of two minds on the whole thing. Ginger is becoming exasperated, although more because of herself than because of Sakiko.

"What would you do if you were I, Sakiko? What if you were widowed, God forbid, and came to the United States, leaving Mai behind with your family? Would you go off for the night with an American man?"

"It depends how nice he is."

"You're kidding!"

"No kidding. If I like him, I do what I want."

"Would you tell Mai?"

"Not until she is older. But if she finds out, it is not end of world."

"I need a beer. How about you?" Ginger is picking up the tab for this meal. She got Sakiko to agree to that before they left the house.

"I have one too." Sakiko signals the waitress.

Tonight, after a week of Japanese dinners, Ginger is more accustomed to eating her rice without seasoning. Now she can enjoy the slight sweetness of it, an unadorned but not flavorless complement to her rich sashimi.

"Wouldn't you feel bad if Mai needed you, and you were off having a good time?" Several issues, independent but overlapping, are occupying Ginger's mind.

"I can have good time."

"But if I wouldn't want my daughter knowing about it, maybe I shouldn't be doing it."

"I don't understand."

"Don't you think it's wrong for me to have one standard for my daughter and another for myself? Would you want Mai dating a married man?"

"Ginger, I can't follow what you say. You are adult. Daughter is not adult."

Sakiko's comment might make most people in Ginger's situation feel better. It has the opposite effect on Ginger. She feels both guilty for what she's doing and stupid for what she's worrying about, but, she begins to think, if she *is* stupid, wouldn't her stupidity vitiate her guilt? Wouldn't it mean she can't reason properly due to lack of intelligence?

"I'm worried Bernie will need me when I'm not reachable. It will be the weekend in Nether Gorge too, you know." Ginger has moved on to a different anxiety, a new point of departure. She'd wanted to cancel her Japanese trip when Bernie flunked chemistry, but Bernie and Reggie assured Ginger everything would be fine at home.

"Your sister will look after her."

"Yes, but I've never taken off like this before."

"Taken off?"

"You know, gone with a man. A married man."

"She will need you because of that?" Sakiko eats the last grain of rice in her bowl. "Is problem Akira-san married, or you are not married with Akira-san?"

"Both. My faith," Ginger says, adding yet another layer of analysis, "doesn't allow for ruining marriages." *Or for ruined ones,* she adds to herself.

"Any religion doesn't think that is good idea. But people are human." Sakiko drains her beer. "You should enjoy weekend. Your sister manage at home. Awaji is not so far from Osaka. You are good mother, but you need to be yourself too, not just mother."

"Maybe you're right."

"And when you cross bridge between city and island, look for ship hanging in water."

"A hanging ship?"

"If day is misty, you cannot see horizon. Ship looks like hanging in grey between water and sky."

Better the ship hangs than Ginger.

Thursday, July 13

I'm not as good a woman as I look.

That's what I should have said to Sakiko over dinner tonight, after I told her about Akira's invitation in the north hallway. Is everyone thinking I'm a loose woman? Maybe I am a loose woman. No, that's not possible, not after all these years of behaving myself. It's just that nothing like this has ever happened to me before. I've always been in control of my emotions. I will say with all my resolve: *Nothing is going to happen on Awaji Island.* I'm interested in earthquakes and seeing a bit of Japan. That's it.

At any rate, Sakiko and I continued our girl talk on the train ride back from Dotonbori. She said Hiro has had flings but nothing serious. She accepts that as something Hiro occasionally does. I couldn't bring myself to ask her if she has reciprocated. She seemed surprised to hear I wouldn't have put up with behavior like that from Steve. She made a point of saying Hiro's a good husband. I couldn't tell if she was protesting too much or if she believes what she says. I've heard Japanese wives are more passive than American wives, but perhaps that's just a stereotype. I regretted I'd commented on my own expectations about marital fidelity; I don't want her to think I was second-guessing her judgment.

We also talked about children. Sakiko said Akira's wife had been desperate for a child but that she abandoned her hopes years ago when doctors told her she couldn't conceive. Akira became more aloof to his wife after that, Sakiko said. This all makes me feel worse, but why I'm not sure. It's not as though I'm taking advantage—although people might think I am, or will—of another woman's misery. I asked Sakiko if Megumi is a friend of hers. She said no, that Megumi keeps to her friends from childhood and people from her job. She doesn't like to socialize with the faculty spouses, especially since she's given up on children. I asked about adoption. Sakiko said adopting isn't done much in Japan. Somehow Sakiko seems to know everything there is to know about all the teachers' lives. (And I thought Confederate was gossipy!) This makes me uncomfortable, like I'm an open book for people to read. I can't imagine they don't all know what's going on with Akira and me, even though nothing is going on. It looks like there is, though, which is just as bad—the appearance of impropriety can be as damning as impropriety itself. I should have told Akira I wouldn't go to Awaji.

Back to children—Sakiko said Hiro would have liked another child, a son, she said, but she has been perfectly content with Mai. I had to admit to her that I sometimes wish for another child. Its gender wouldn't matter. There's some part of me that's not finished with childbearing and childrearing. If there had been an eligible man, things would have been different for me.

Sakiko asked if I like appearing married, wearing my ring. I didn't know what to say. I'm afraid I wear the ring for the wrong reason—not to signify my continuing connection to my husband, for I'm a realist, I know I'm no longer married, but to put men off, to turn them away. It doesn't always have that effect, though. Many men seem happy to horn in on another man's wife. They are men who don't want a wife, just a lay. Of course, men who don't want a wife would approach me whether I wear the ring or not, so it's rather a moot point. What I like about the ring is that it shows I have been married, that I've lived a committed life with a man, that I'm a person to be taken seriously. I never thought about it before, but the ring, and my marriage, give me credibility that I may not otherwise have. It's interesting what symbols say.

My thoughts are troubled thoughts. I'm troubled by what I am doing, and I'm troubled by what I'm not doing. I'm ready to find someone to move into my later years with, someone who will be my opera companion, who will make a cheerful grandfather and then a reassuring nurse or consolable patient when the time comes. I don't care if he's good in bed; I'm past the point where that matters. I want someone to smile at me in the morning, help me change the sheets, and celebrate my birthday with a little box of costume jewelry.

I'm getting way ahead of myself with Akira, but his marital status makes me think about my limited options. Once Bernie's on her own, I may want to settle down with someone, before I'm so old that no one will want me. I want both to see my loved ones in heaven and to be married to a man I love and who loves me. Are these wishes mutually exclusive? If I fall in love with and marry someone who's divorced, I'll be excommunicated for marrying a man the Church considers still married. If only my church didn't restrict me so!

The immediate problem with Akira is that I could be a home wrecker. (It burns me up that it's women, not men, who are referred to as *home wreckers*.) On the other hand, if he's miserable in his marriage, wouldn't I be doing both him and Megumi a favor? But what sort of crazy rationalization is that?

One would think Akira had asked for my hand.

I told Sakiko about Akira waltzing me around the music room. She couldn't believe it. She said Akira isn't "typical Japanese man." He doesn't behave like a Japanese man, she said. I believe her. It doesn't even sound like something my American male colleagues would do, although it might be something they would fantasize. Some of us act on our fantasies; some of us don't.

I've been dragging my feet about calling Ken. Sakiko suggested I call him tonight, but now it's too late. I don't know what to say to him. Why would Ken want to hear from me? And why am I interested in him? Or am I? He's probably married with a couple of perfect children and a perky wife who loves to cook.

People think I'm so prim and proper. They have ultrahigh expectations of me. Don't they know I have needs too?

Friday, July 14

Hiro and Sakiko have gone out to a nightclub—Sakiko wants to dance. Hiro didn't look happy during dinner, didn't say a word. He smoked while we were eating, while *he* was eating. I bet that was to insult Sakiko's cooking.

Before dinner Sakiko and I visited the neighborhood graveyard—we walked through a few streets in their development and then across the main road and deep into a tree-lined older neighborhood, the neighborhood Hiro grew up in. Eventually we left even those narrow streets and older houses behind. We traveled far along gravel paths and dense brush until we came to a clearing. It was there that Hiro's parents were laid to rest. Visually I took in the mass of graves, or whatever the word is for where ashes are inurned. Small stone markers, white, gray, and graying. Sakiko set out crackers for the dead, a full box that looked like it held the Japanese equivalent of Ritz crackers. It struck me as superstitious, this obsession with feeding the dead, but upon reflection it's no stranger, I suppose, than a Catholic's attachment to a relic.

Today I attended a meeting in the conference room. (I was glad not to see the chairs of the principal's office again.) This was a meeting of the exchange committee, and I sat at the foot of the table, the principal at its head, or maybe I was at the head and he at the foot. In either case, all eyes were on me. The upholstered seat felt hot. There is an air conditioner in that room, but the air it was giving off was tepid, lifeless. The committee consists of at least a dozen people: principal, assistant principal, Mrs. Kitajima on behalf of the PTA, a teacher from each of the disciplines, and a couple of other people, older men in suits, but I didn't catch who they were. Teru, the only full-time art teacher, sat at my right hand, having greeted me by shaking my hand and patting me on the back. During the meeting he drew caricatures of everyone at the table. My likeness, which he made a point of showing me while the principal was talking, was of a woman in an evening dress. I looked remarkably like Sargent's Madame X. Does Teru know that the real Madame X and I share a given name?

For the entire hour the meeting ran, I felt as if I was trying to dock a boat in a gale. One of the teachers asked me about Confederate High's "culture." He wondered how "liberal" it is, how well supervised our students are on field trips, for instance, and whether something he'd heard was true—that students kissed in the hallways. His English was a struggle for him. I had the sense, from his glancing down at his notes throughout his questioning, from his halting speech, and from the sweat on his forehead, that he'd either practiced his questions beforehand or wished he had.

I was at a loss because of course some of the kids do kiss in the hallways, some grope, too. I said the students are well-supervised, that we have hall monitors at all times (I didn't say they are usually students themselves), and that I'd never heard of any problems in the hallways. But why would I? I keep my nose in my books, I avoid faculty meetings, I toss Walk's newsletter in the wastebasket unread. What was the Confederate committee thinking of when they chose me for this job? That ignorance is bliss? They may have deployed a secret weapon sending *me* here. My ignorance may in fact serve Confederate well.

Then another teacher, another man (Mrs. K. and I were the only women present), asked if we have metal detectors at our school doors. I said no and added that we have our own police officer in the school all day, every day. I thought this would be reassuring, but my comment prompted plenty of chair-scooching across the carpet, a good deal of air sucking, many exchanged looks, and much rustling of papers. I hurried to add that the officer was there more as a counselor than as a law-enforcer, although this isn't strictly true. I told the group that each of the schools in the county has its own police officer. Finally, I said we preferred people to machines, that we treat our students as maturing individuals who have many opportunities to learn right from wrong. I think I lost most of them with that near-tautology. Silence fell over the city.

Akira, sitting midway down the table, broke the hush by asking about Confederate's music program. Because this is something I know a lot about, I spent fifteen minutes citing our three orchestras (two strings only and one full orchestra—with woodwinds, brass, and percussion), three jazz bands, an award-winning marching band, two glee clubs (lost them with "glee," except for Akira, who caught my eye and nodded encouragingly), the a cappella group, and a "big band" dance band. I described our musical performances occurring throughout the year—including the fall and spring musicals, our state-of-the-art auditorium, our faculty of two full-time and three part-time music teachers, our booster clubs, our fundraising successes from parent-chaperoned car washes (which thin, tanned, long-haired girls advertise by standing on street corners in teeny short-shorts and halter tops, waving cardboard signs at motorists, thereby presaging or imitating streetwalkers—but I left all that out), and our annual trips to the Kennedy Center, Carnegie Hall, and various European destinations. I killed a lot of time talking about my love, music. By the time I was finished, the teachers had to get back to their classes.

I've gotten into a rhythm at school—observing classes, speaking to groups, and spending a lot of time in the library, in the cushy armchairs that are scattered about and are off-limits to students. The library is light and airy and high-ceilinged, and often I roam the stacks, pretending I can read Japanese books. I sit and look at them, slowly turning the pages back to front, hoping to make people think I'm picking up the language. It's not so different from flipping through a fashion magazine backwards, as I do in the grocery store's check-out line. There just aren't any pictures in the library books, and I can't understand a word of what I'm looking at. I can *imagine* what is said, though, which is even more interesting. I make up stories to go with the ideographs.

In the library, after a while, especially in the long afternoons, I get sleepy, and several times I've awakened to find a group of schoolgirls, over by the globe, pretending not to be looking in my direction. I've been casual about wiping the wetness from the side of my face, passing my hand over my cheek as if I were rubbing an itchy spot. I feel the way Esther Summerson looked in my dream, as if I were in a fish bowl, everyone watching what I'm doing.

I finished Greene and have started on a new book, new for me, that is—*The Damnation of Theron Ware*. It's about a (married) Methodist minister in upstate New York who has a bizarre, one-sided thing going with the organist from the Catholic church in town. The book would make a good opera. I keep rereading Chapter XXII. I hear two different musical styles in that Adirondack forest. Protestant revival hymns rise from one clearing, dance tunes of Catholic carousers pour out from the other, and there is poor Theron, trying to keep a foot in both camps. It's interesting to see a nineteenth-century author's description of Celia's sensuality and Monsignor Forbes's intellectuality, and the hyper-stimulation Theron deals with because of them.

I had an e-mail from His Eminence today—he wants to be sure everything is going well. He asked me to rate how well Confederate and I were being received here, on a scale of one to ten. What's that supposed to mean? How *I* am being received? He could have put it better; his diction was as sloppy as ever. He could have asked me how well we're suited to each other as schools, or even what I think the chances are the Japanese will want the partnership, based on what I've observed so far. Well, I fixed his wagon. I told him I thought we were coming in at a five. What can he do to me? Will my behavior here affect my chances of winning the partnership, negatively affect them, that is? Probably. Do I care? Not at this moment.

I also had a note from the *Post* reporter, which I'm going to pretend I didn't get. She wants an update and said she plans to run a big spread when I get back. I hope that's only if I come back victorious. She asked for a picture of me here—at the school, with another teacher, at a historic site. I have my new digital camera with me—haven't used it yet. I don't know how it works and don't like to take pictures anyway. I was hoping to get back home without using it. Well, I can pack it for the trip tomorrow. Maybe Akira will help. Guys like to do that kind of thing, appear competent, that is.

Unbelievable! I've just come back upstairs, having made an innocent trip down to check out the kitchen in search of something to eat. I had taken a sedative after

Sakiko and Hiro left, to get me through the night (I'll go home a drug addict, if I'm not already one) and my altered state left me with the munchies. Xanax breaks down my eating inhibitions at the same time it calms me. So I looked in the freezer for ice cream. Finding none, I looked in the fridge for leftovers from our pork cutlet dinner. We must have eaten everything at dinner. I looked in the produce drawer and found oranges but was afraid to eat one; everything is so dear here. I did find a long, skinny cucumber in there, but I wanted something fatty, salty, or sweet, not something nutritious. Sakiko shops every day, which means there's not much sitting around in the refrigerator. I searched the cupboards, taking a drink of Sakiko's special liqueur and coming upon a box of crackers like the ones we left at the cemetery. I ate a bunch of those.

All of that is hardly worth mentioning. What was *shocking* was that as I passed the darkened pillow room, the one the Murakamis use for special purposes, I heard noises coming from it. The only light nearby was in the stairwell, and it wasn't shedding much light into the hallway. I thought maybe a burglar had broken in, and it took all my will and courage to take a few steps backward so I could see into the room. Slowly I moved my face around the corner of the open doorway, just enough to see the movement on the floor, among the pillows. I wondered if the burglar was searching under the pillows, under floorboards, for valuables. And then I heard the noises again—two peoples' voices, soft utterings, one high, the other higher, and their sounds were sighs. At least they were at first. I stood stuck to the floor, not wanting to startle them or to embarrass them if they heard or saw me. To be perfectly honest, though, I must confess I was a voyeur at that moment, at that terrible, lovely moment, for I could have walked away, I could have moved unnoticed. I shouldn't have stayed, I know that, but I couldn't move, or put more honestly, I didn't choose to move. The sighs grew longer and deeper until they were moans, and the moving mass was more measured, more rhythmic, a coupling of nocturnal creatures, not thrashing about, but melting, one into the other. The sound, though, more than the sight, was what stirred me, what nearly made me shudder. They were sucking sounds, breaths heavy with urging, murmurs filled with a fever of love.

As the moment passed and the bodies collapsed one on the other, the noises fell to the sweetest of teasings, of lovers' talk, and it was then that I realized whose lovemaking I'd witnessed, whose privacy I had intruded upon. And I was even more ashamed of myself than if I had watched two adults making love. It was Mai in the pillow room, Mai with another girl, and they had been wholly intimate and wholly abandoned to each other, and all the while I had been watching them.

I was wrong when I wrote only yesterday that sex isn't important to me. It's clear my body craves something that my mind can't deal with. If Akira were here now and asked me to dance, or if he were sitting next to me on a piano bench, singing me a love song, I could not, I *would* not, do the right thing. I would abandon myself to him.

Saturday, July 15

I'm writing this from my room at the *ryokan* on Awaji Island. I'm going to set down dialogue as faithfully as I can. It goes without saying I haven't used a tape recorder, so I wouldn't be able put my hand on a Bible and swear that the quotations are verbatim. Nonetheless, they do convey the sense of the speakers.

I spent the morning with Reiko, Akira's voice student. We were working on her pronunciation. Ten minutes into the lesson, she moved us off course.

"*Sensei*, may I ask you a question?"

I nodded.

"Mother think I should not date until I am eighteen. You have daughter. Is she allowed date?"

I wondered how she'd heard about Bernie. "Different cultures and different parents have their own ways of doing things," I said. "Of making those important decisions."

"But I think mother old-fashioned. In America, high school girl not date?"

I knew I'd be more comfortable answering her questions from a teacher's perspective rather than from a parent's. "Many girls date before they're eighteen," I told her, wondering which American girls haven't begun by then, "but it's not good to start too early. Some girls are ready for the responsibility, and some aren't." I didn't mention that Bernie's been dating since she started high school. That's when Mother let me date. How she lived through my girlhood I don't know, but lucky for her she had my dad going through it with her.

"How do you know if girl is ready?" Reiko tapped her pencil, already a conductor.

"That's what parents are for. And whether the boy is responsible is important, too."

"Responsible?"

Her questions were taking us far from our work. "Mature enough to be interested in someone else's good," I told her, "and not just his own. I'd apply that test to the girl, too."

"Does American girl have sex with boyfriend?"

I was amazed at Reiko's frankness. Do I have a reputation here as an itinerant sex adviser? "Some do, some don't," I said, then turned the tables. "What is it like here?"

"Sort of same. What I hear." Like Bernie's comment about not having sex, Reiko depersonalized the issue. But then I did that too.

We returned to our drills. I was unnerved and had a feeling Reiko had heard of my plans for the night. I kept my eye on the classroom clock. It looked back at me.

A little while later, Reiko said, "How was wedding?"

"Mine? It rained all day."

"You wear big white dress?"

"A white dress, with a blue satin sash tied in a bow in the back. My mother made my dress. I looked like Little Bo Peep."

"Rock singer?"

"A character from a children's song. With the sheep she loses, I mean, without the sheep she loses." I offered Rciko a piece of gum.

"Chewing gum is not allowed at school," she said as she popped a piece in her mouth. "I want Western wedding. No white kimono. Only time woman wear white kimono, she married or buried."

"Your diction is very good, Reiko," I said, "but let's get back to working on your pronunciation."

At noon Akira came for me. Reiko thanked me, bowed to both of us, and backed out of the room. Akira and I walked out the front door of the school just as the other teachers were leaving. They nodded to us. I felt conspicuous carrying a tote bag, although how would they know it had a change of clothes in it? I also felt conspicuous for my lack of hose, which I'd worn all week to keep Sakiko happy. Today was different though, and Sakiko understood that I didn't want to have my legs wrapped up in hot hosiery for the trip. She'd surprised me by encouraging me to go to school barelegged.

In Akira's tiny car, only the space of the gear shift separated us. Akira had picked up lunch for us at a convenience store, so we stopped at a rest area along the highway to eat. Cart vendors had hot food for sale, and I looked it over on my way to the restroom, recognizing none of it. In the clean, modern women's room all the Japanese-style toilets, those ceramic ovals in the ground, were occupied, so I used the Western style. Now that I have the hang of dropping my underwear to my ankles and crouching on my haunches, I'm finding the Japanese toilet more comfortable in a public place—I don't have to do the toilet hover, trying at all costs not to touch the seat. True to form, there were neither paper towels nor hand dryers in the restroom, although there was plenty of soap. I got everything in my purse wet as I dug for Sakiko's little terry-cloth towel.

We walked along a path from the parking lot to a grassy spot at the foot of the hill. Akira spread out a blanket and we took our shoes off. He sat cross-legged, and I knelt facing him, then sat back on my legs the way I've seen Japanese women do. That hurt after a few minutes, so I resettled, cross-legged, my flowered skirt covering all but my bare feet.

Akira opened his cooler and drew out plastic-wrapped *onigiri*. Before today I'd never had those yummy rice balls. The ones he'd bought were filled with pickled plum and salmon and wrapped in dried seaweed. The rice was sticky and not as soft as when it's straight from the cooker; it was also slightly sweet, the inside ingredients a little salty. I ate three onigiri. Akira never took his eyes off me, as though he found something fascinating in my biting, chewing, and swallowing. I drank straight from the bottle the iced coffee he'd bought for me from the vending machine. The drink was sweet and bitter both.

Finally Akira spoke. "For some people, sushi is an aphrodisiac."

I tried to ignore his comment. "What will we see on Awaji?"

"According to Tanizaki, there are thirty-three temples we can visit on Awaji."

"I trust we aren't going to see all of them," I told him, remembering my exhaustion in Kyoto.

"I'm not sure we'll see even one. We'll visit the earthquake museum, drive to our ryokan, have dinner, and enjoy the baths."

"I didn't bring my suit."

"Your suit?"

"My swim suit. I don't have one with me."

"You won't need one."

These words I swear he said, just like that, so casually, with such certainty. Part of me was aghast, but more of me was interested to learn what would happen next, as though this was someone else's story.

"Tomorrow, on our way home, we can stop in Kobe. I know a gallery there that's showing work of Watanabe Sadao."

"Who?"

"A printmaker. He put Jesus and sushi in the same picture. I thought you might like to see his work."

"I would."

"The color of your blouse reminds me of Watanabe."

"This yellow?" I asked. Today I felt insecure in my yellow blouse. It's a lovely Verona yellow, and I'm fond of the color, but yellow is hard for me to wear. I was annoyed, when I'd looked in the restroom mirror, that I'd worn it today, that I'd brought it with me, that I'd bought it in the first place.

Akira was looking off into the trees on the other side of the highway, and it seemed as if he were thousands of miles away. "It's orpiment," he said.

That color, that orpiment, would look better on Akira than on me, but he looked perfect just as he was, in a geranium-red golf shirt. As others have done, I like to pinch geranium leaves and then put my fingers to my nose, breathing in the spice. When I deadhead marigolds in my garden, I sniff each blossom before I drop it in my trug. Other people have herb gardens for cooking; mine's for smelling. I wanted to pinch Akira to find out if he smells as good as he looks. Not only that, but I'd like to know what excuse he gave his wife for his absence tonight.

Back in the car, we hurried through the urban tangle, and I tried to picture how Japanese cities must have looked at the beginning of this century—smoky and filled with low, flat buildings, I imagined. In the present, the roadbed between Osaka and Kobe hemmed us in. Tall, homely buildings and electrical wires trapped the traffic racing past, cars and trucks driven by people rushing to escape a monster's clutches. My eyes stung from the steel shine of the motor vehicles, the glare of the silver and white buildings, the blurry bullets of trains. Around us were a million mirrors, the asphalt road seething beneath us.

Tunnels began to arrive in quick succession, my eyes not adjusting to the dark before we were through one, back into the sunshine, and then into another dark, narrow space. Brief and unrelenting, the tunnels made the road seem more below ground than above it. Akira smoked with the windows cracked an inch or two, the air conditioning on. He hummed the score from the first act of *La Bohème* as we made our way.

"Ginger, has it ever occurred to you that entering a tunnel is like looking into someone's mouth?"

It took me a while to reply, and I was nervous asking the question, but I needed to talk about it. I needed to know.

"Did you know my husband was killed in a tunnel?"

"Ginger, I'm sorry. Of course I didn't know."

"You know I'm a widow?"

"Hiro mentioned it."

"At a staff meeting?"

"Why, yes, in fact. Actually over drinks, after a meeting."

"Steve was killed in a tunnel collapse. He was the head engineer on a job. A beam collapsed and he was buried. He died alone."

"I'm sorry. Again." He put the window all the way down and tossed out his cigarette. "I can see how Japan would make you uneasy."

"I feel weird going to an earthquake museum."

"We can skip it."

"No, I'd like to see it. But if I'm quiet, you'll know why."

I looked for the hanging ships in the Akashi Channel as we drove over the bridge between Kobe and Awaji, but it was so bright and clear there was no mistaking the glassy water from the matte sky.

Approaching midpoint on the bridge, Akira asked, "Do you like bridges, Ginger?"

"Usually. More than I like tunnels."

"This bridge is interesting. The 1995 earthquake struck while it was being built. The epicenter of the quake lay between the two towers of the bridge."

"Oh?"

"The towers moved apart by a yard."

"What happened to the people who were on that yard of the bridge?"

"Oh, don't worry, Ginger," he said. "The bridge is built to withstand earthquakes up to eight-and-a-half on the Richter scale."

"What was the rating of the 1995 quake?"

"Seven point two. Six thousand people were killed."

We got out of the car at the far end of the bridge, and, with my camera, Akira took a picture of me with my back to Honshu, the mainland.

The earthquake museum, erected on the fault line, was anticlimactic after the tunnels and bridge. The curators salvaged an on-site building torn apart in the quake and incorporated it into the exhibit itself. Placards around the quake-created trench explained the area's seismography. I was relieved when we left.

The Awaji landscape is hilly and green, drying onions pendent in field sheds, flowering bushes growing beside the roads. We flew up and down narrow roads and through tight crossroads settlements, and here and there I caught sight of the sea. I felt more carefree than I have in a long time. As July days often do, it seemed the day would last forever. I'll never forget the Japanese landscapes I saw on our trip here. I'll never forget how the pastoral life here on Awaji is separated by a thin stretch of water from the hectic build-up back there on the mainland. I'll never forget the mainland, its hillsides cut and then covered over with cement and netting to hold back the rocks. The cement itself resembles rock, but, after studying it, I've figured out it's man-made, fake.

Finally, at one of the intersections, Akira made a sharp left turn, drove a hundred yards farther, then pulled into a parking lot and turned off the engine. He opened his door and came around and opened mine. He took a small black case out of the trunk.

"Is this the ryokan?"

"It is."

Before we reached it, a woman wearing a kimono opened the door of the rambling, two-story wooden building. Akira and she exchanged greetings like old friends. Akira introduced her to me as the manager of the inn. I bowed to her, but she bowed lower to me. Akira and I left our shoes at the door and put on cotton slippers. The manager led the way down a short hall and up steep stairs. She stopped in front of an open doorway. Akira was behind me. The woman removed her slippers and entered a room. I followed her in while Akira waited in the hall. She spoke to me in Japanese and I understood not a word she said. Soon she left, spoke to Akira in the hall, and went back the way we'd come. I stood at the door of my room.

"Your maid's name is Yuki, Ginger. She'll be here shortly."

"Is she your maid too?"

"Yes, but first she'll take care of you."

"Where is your room?"

"Right here, across the hall from yours."

I left him and turned back to look at my room. The tatami mats on the floor give off a boggy pungency, a fragrance that is to me still strange yet not unpleasant. A small table and two legless chairs (only cushioned seats and backs) sit in the middle of the room. Built-in closets and an alcove line one wall. In the alcove are an *ikebana* flower arrangement and a hanging scroll with a picture of a fish on it.

"There's no bed," I observed, aloud, to no one.

Just then Yuki bowed into my room with a small tray of tea and one sweet bean cake. She set the tray on the table and opened a sliding closet door, directing my attention, in Japanese, to the futon.

I heard Akira again from the hallway, "Another maid will make the bed up for you when it's time."

Yuki opened a built-in drawer and pointed to the lightweight cotton kimono, indigo and white, folded neatly inside the drawer. Sakiko had told me about the *yukata*—I can wear it around the ryokan, even into the public areas, and I can sleep in it. Yuki showed me, gesturing with her small, graceful hands, how to use the remote control for the air conditioner and how to latch my sliding door. Oystershell-like paper panels run down its length.

I hung my change of clothes in my room then took a few minutes to wash in the communal women's room, changing into the pink plastic slippers left at the door. Back in my room, I sat down to have my tea and cake and make these notes. I haven't heard any sound from across the hall. Akira's door is closed, although I've left mine open.

NINE

Shiso

Ginger rises and slides her door shut, undressing down to her bra and panties. She unfolds the yukata, slips it on, and ties the fabric belt as Sakiko showed her. In the drawer with the yukata is a black hip-length jacket, which she hangs over the back of a chair. She pushes her room door into its pocket and puts her feet back into her slippers, which Yuki set with the toes facing the hallway.

Ginger knocks on the frame of Akira's door, and he calls for her to come in. He is sitting in his room in a yukata that matches Ginger's, his eyes closed. Ginger stands in the doorway, and he gets up and comes to meet her, examining her, beginning at her throat, moving past her ruby-studded Greek cross on its gold chain, and settling on her chest.

"Is something wrong?" Ginger asks.

"Your yukata is closed backwards."

"I couldn't remember whether Sakiko said it was right over left or left over right."

"It's left over right. Think of your heart as being on top."

"Like wearing your heart on your sleeve?"

"You could look at it that way. Would you like to go for a walk around the grounds? The heat of the day has passed."

"Should I get the jacket?"

"Leave *haori* in your room. It's still too warm for a jacket."

Ginger isn't thinking about the jacket for warmth but for propriety.

At the door to the gardens they change shoes again, this time into geta, blocky wooden sandals with downy black thongs for their toes. Two bars of wood attached to the soles of the shoes raise the foot beds off the ground. The toe thong is threaded through in the middle of the geta, so Ginger's little toes hang off the sides of the platforms. She mentions that this seems to be a design flaw. Akira tells her that if the thongs were attached asymmetrically, the backs of the geta would run into each other as she walks. Ginger isn't confident walking in these shoes, but at least hers aren't as treacherously high as Akira's. He walks as though he had been born in them.

The couple wanders through the gardens, returning to find Yuki laying out their dinner in Akira's room. She brings in dozens of dishes, each with a few bites of food on it. Akira tells Ginger the meal is *kaiseki ryori*, a special party meal meant to appeal to all the senses. Ginger eats her way through slabs of sashimi, *soba* noodles, grated vegetables, grilled fish, and salad, as if her last meal had been days ago. Accenting the sashimi is daikon radish and a jagged-edged leaf from the *shiso* plant. Finding the shiso's citrus-cinnamon flavor much to her liking, Ginger rolls up a leaf and eats the whole thing at once. Akira, meanwhile, slurps his noodles in the Japanese style, his eyes on Ginger. Ginger tries five different sauces and pronounces all of them salty, which doesn't mean she won't eat them. Yuki has set the rice out in a lacquered bowl with a lid, and they save it until the end, when Yuki serves soup and pickles. They polish off a bottle of chilled sake and three oversized bottles of beer.

"Are you sure you've had enough to eat, Ginger?"

Ginger sets down her chopsticks. "I've never met a food I didn't like."

They peel and eat oranges for dessert as they drink their tea. While Yuki clears the table, they sit in the corner of Akira's room where the floor is hardwood and there's a pair of Western-style chairs, a coffee table between them. They talk of teaching, of literature.

"Have you read *The Good Soldier*?" Ginger asks.

Akira takes a drag on his first postprandial cigarette. "I don't know it."

"That's a story I enjoy teaching, but my students hate it. They say nothing happens in it."

"Kids like scenes that last six seconds. What else?"

"*Sister Carrie*, which my students think is going to be about a nun, and *Portrait of an Artist*. My students complain about reading *Portrait*, thinking it irrelevant, but usually, eventually, they identify with Stephen Dedalus and his efforts to shrug off his Irish Catholic heritage."

"What's it like to teach a work with so much religion in it?"

"The non-Catholics are interested in an unfamiliar religion, and the Catholics are surprised at how their religion used to be practiced."

"Why do you like literature from that period?" Akira asks.

"The risks that writers were taking in the second half of the nineteenth century and the effects their works had on the writers who followed them, that's what excites me about that age. Writers explored new styles, new techniques, new themes. They explored realism, which happens to be my favorite cultural movement. It was a time of explosive growth in literature, unique in history."

"The stories start very slowly, don't they? Many Japanese novels of that time period are also that way."

"I like them *because* they start slowly," Ginger says. "It gives me time to prepare for what's to come. I could drown in the sensuousness of Henry James' words. His commas caress my arms and legs as I read." Ginger might express herself a little less candidly in Akira's company.

"You'd like *Suna no Onna. Woman in the Dunes.* How many ways could you describe a grain of sand?"

"That sounds slow!"

"Slow but powerful."

"Is this another story about a man thinking of divorcing his wife?" Ginger asks.

"No, about one trapped in a house that's buried in the dunes."

"His own house?"

"A widow's house."

They go on like this until the sky is dark, Akira telling Ginger how a production of *Pagliacci* inspired him to compose a one-act opera based on "Han's Crime," Han a knife thrower who kills his wife during a performance. Akira has written the music and is looking for a librettist. Ginger tells Akira how she hears music as she reads, as in what she read last night, the passage in which Ware stalks the woman with whom he's infatuated. He is following her to New York City, and Ginger heard music as she read about the minister heading south by train along the Hudson River, music for an unwritten opera. All these things they speak of together, as if the people in the stories were a part of their own innermost lives.

A maid arrives and makes up Akira's futon. Akira asks Ginger how she feels about the school partnership. She wonders aloud if perhaps Akira no longer appears objective because he has developed a friendship with her; she suggests he consider disqualifying himself from the committee. Akira assures her he can recuse himself if necessary but that he shouldn't need to. He talks at length about the advantages the partnership has for his school— the cultural richness of the northern Virginia area, Confederate's academic achievements, its diverse course offerings, and the prestige of its music program. Akira's enthusiasm and commitment allow Ginger to regain some of her determination to win the partnership.

"I could visit you, Ginger. Every year we would send two teachers for several weeks. And you could visit us."

"Us?"

"The Murakami family and me."

The midnight hour has nearly come, and Akira says they should enjoy the baths before any more time passes.

Ginger re-enters her room a little nervous. The maid has prepared her futon, placing the head of it against the alcove. Ginger pushes it cockeyed, angling the head toward the windows. She removes her undergarments and puts the yukata back on. When she goes out into the hallway, Akira is waiting for her. It's still unclear whether they will be bathing together. They cross a short, covered exterior walkway and enter a low-slung wooden building.

Inside the bathhouse, the foyer is dimly lit. Akira motions for Ginger to enter the door on the left. He takes the right-hand door. The door closes behind Ginger, and she rounds a corner, past wooden benches bolted to the floor, then into the dazzle of glossy yellow wall tiles, their brilliance broken by the sky-blue plastic floor mats through which water will drain to the foundation. Shower heads and hand sprayers line the wall, a stack of pink plastic stools standing guard at one end, a counter of fluffy white towels at the other. Through the arched doorway at the far side of the shower room is found the most important room, the bathing room itself, and in the very center of it sits a tile-lined sunken tub, filled with blue water. Ginger is alone here in this bathing complex. Except for the door she used to enter the bath and an emergency door to the exterior of the building, there is no other door. She won't be bathing with Akira after all.

Ginger sheds her yukata and leaves it on a bench. Ignoring the stack of stools, she turns the taps for the middle shower and uses the liquid in the dispenser to wash her face, hair, and body. She rinses with cool water and uses her hands, in short strokes, to press the water from her hair. She turns and makes the short walk to the pool, slipping in along the submerged steps and wading to the far edge. The hot water sends a chill through her, goose bumps forming on her flesh, her nipples firming with the shock. In the dimness of the wall sconces she sits to soak, shutting her eyes and thinking over all that has happened this day.

She may have dozed, but in any case, after some time, Ginger hears deep voices and the spritzing of shower water. When she opens her eyes, two portly, middle-aged men are progressing toward the pool, white towels tucked at their waists. One of them is limping. Their faces flushed, they are speaking loudly in Japanese. Ginger looks away as they drop their towels and back their way down the steps. Soon their voices become quieter, and Ginger glances their way. They are seated next to the steps. They nod at her, and she nods back. Their towels are behind their head, at the side of the pool. Ginger didn't bother to pick up a towel. Now she's stuck in the bath.

The best thing would be for Ginger to outlast the men, but she's had a good ten minutes' start on them and probably isn't as accustomed as the men are to the extreme heat of the Japanese bath. It isn't long before she is physically uncomfortable. The men have stopped talking; their eyes are closed. Meanwhile Ginger is growing hotter and hotter.

Keeping her shoulders at water level, Ginger edges toward the stairs, slowly, so as not to roil the surface and call attention to herself. When she arrives at the steps, the men still have their eyes closed. Ginger must choose: she could make a mad dash up the steps and climb out quickly but run the risk of having the sounds and splashes call the men's attention to her, or she could inch her way up and out, prolonging her exposure but decreasing her chances of being observed.

Taking a middle ground, Ginger walks out of the pool. She does it in a smooth, sophisticated fashion. She doesn't look back.

Akira is waiting for her in the foyer. "How was your bath?" he asks.

"Fine, but where were you?"

"In the men's bath. Where else would I have been?"

"That's odd. There were men in my bath."

"Two men, one limping?"

"That's right. Why?"

"I saw them earlier. They're drunk. They got the wrong bath."

The couple walks back in silence, pausing at their doors.

"Well, goodnight then. Thank you for the lovely day." Ginger bows slightly to Akira.

"The pleasure was mine, Ginger." He bows lower. Surely he's not mocking her!

Ginger enters her room and stands facing the hall. Akira turns and enters his room. It seems, finally, that there is nothing more to this than two teachers on a trip. Ginger shuts but doesn't latch her door.

The moonlight from a waxing, nearly full moon flickers through the shoji at the windows. Sliding back the paper screen, Ginger looks for the man in the moon. Tonight he looks more like an old woman, a hag. After Ginger returns to the States, the moon will be a new moon, a darker circle in a dark sky. Like a mother, the moon is always there, even when we don't see her. This is also true of Ginger's God.

Ginger removes her yukata once more and, forsaking her nightgown, drops naked to the futon. She has shut off the air conditioning and opened the windows, and the air in the room is turning moist and warm. The sheets are smooth and light against her skin, but the pillow is filled with buckwheat hulls, and Ginger finds the lumps disagreeable. Even so, she is asleep within minutes.

❧   ❧

Ginger hears a noise in the hallway and stirs from her dream. She and Steve were once more on their honeymoon in Italy, but this time they were attending the weekly papal audience. Their pastor had arranged for them to receive a special blessing from the pontiff, so they were seated in the front row with the other newlyweds. At the end of the audience they were to meet His Holiness personally. Ginger was wearing her wedding dress, and the sash was missing. She tried to focus on God as the pope prayed aloud into his microphone for the thousands assembled to hear, but she couldn't concentrate. All she could think was, "I'm going to meet the pope, and something's not right."

Ginger wakes to find that Akira is next to her, kneeling on the mat alongside her futon. He is wearing his yukata, open to the waist. The moonlight falls on the left side of his face and onto his shoulder. Ginger pulls back the sheet and sits up to make space for Akira, heedless of her nakedness. Akira tosses aside her pillow.

"I hate these authentic things," he says, and his mouth is upon hers.

Ginger takes Akira's lips, then his tongue, into her mouth. She tastes his cigarettes and feels the warmth and intensity of his body. His coarse hair, for the first time to her eyes loose from his ponytail, tickles her face, her neck, her chest. His tobacco, his hair upon her, his full-lipped kisses, kisses that she sinks into—these are all new sensations for her.

They kiss for some time, a dalliance, but there is an urgency in both of them that kissing won't satisfy. When Akira kneels and unties his yukata, letting it fall to the foot of the futon, Ginger can't help but compare him with Steve, a man who was powerfully built, hairy-chested, with big arms and thick, callused hands. Akira's chest is hairless, his torso and arms muscular but lean. His musician's hands are soft, his face soft to the touch too, as if he shaved before coming to Ginger. He is different, alien to her experience.

Akira lowers himself onto Ginger, and she wraps her arms around his shoulders, enfolding him in her hungry embrace. Ah, Ginger, wake yourself up! See what you're doing before it's too late! Ginger intertwines her legs with Akira's, her feet with his. Her fingers stroke the fine, short hairs on the back of his neck. She is a lily, opening herself to the sun.

"Ginger, I need you. I want you."

Is Akira the lover Ginger has waited all these barren years for, the man who will mean everything to her, the man for whom she would give her life, the way she would have given her life for Steve O'Neill? Or is this man only making the most of an opportunity that has come his way, discovering an attractive American woman who can feed him intellectually, emotionally, and physically, but for whom he would not, could not, give his entire self—his past, his present, and his future? The pair has spoken of everything but their own lives. Which of them has put up the barriers?

"And I want you," she replies, but her own words bring Ginger up short, her wakefulness overtaking her slumber, for now, not too late, she is recalling her lessons from school, morality lessons, lessons on love. This act, this adult act, was taught as a response not to wanting or needing, but as a way of giving oneself to one's beloved, within marriage, within the cultural norms of monogamy and commitment. Surely Ginger's not the only person left in the world who feels this way. Surely these mores are still taught.

Ginger's mind is now in the ascendancy, and she is suppressing her bodily yearnings. She will not be a means to a man's goal. She deserves to be the goal itself. Akira has pledged himself to another woman, not to Ginger.

Akira's marriage is an unspoken topic between them. They are refusing to be honest with each other.

"We must stop."

Their lovemaking had progressed to the point at which a reasonable person, given the circumstances, the maturity of the individuals, and the feelings between them, would have expected consummation. But now Akira withdraws from the intimacy of Ginger's body and lies supine on the futon beside her, pulling his knees to his chest, wrapping his arms around his legs.

"What's wrong, Ginger? Was I hurting you?"

"No, you weren't hurting me. Not physically, at least."

"How was I hurting you?"

"What we are doing is wrong."

Ginger turns her head to look at this man beside her. She can see his eyelashes in the moonlight. She can't see into his eyes, though, even though they are open. He is looking at the ceiling.

"You have a commitment to your wife, not to me."

"How do you know what my commitment is? Don't you want my love, Ginger? Don't you feel we are meant to be together?"

"I don't do everything I want to do." Ginger looks toward the windows. The moon has moved. "You are the first man I've been intimate with since my husband died."

Akira turns to her.

"Are you surprised?" she asks, closing her eyes. It would be easier if he weren't looking at her.

"I didn't know, one way or the other. I couldn't tell. I didn't want to think about it. Look at me, Ginger."

She opens her eyes.

"Why are you so worried about my marriage?"

"Because where I'm from marriages are important."

"And you don't think they're important here, too?"

"That's my point."

"No," Akira sighs, "the point is that each marriage, each relationship, is different. Surely that's true in the United States. I *know* that's true, Ginger."

"You're right. I don't mean to sound naive. It's just that I personally place faith in marriage."

"In the institution of marriage, or in each marriage individually?"

"Probably more in the institution, in the idea of it as the basis of society, the home for the children we bring into the world."

"I can't argue with that," Akira says, "but what do you think about a particular marriage, if it's a place where love can't grow, or even exist?"

"I don't know what to think. That's beyond my experience."

"Lucky woman."

"What's wrong with your marriage, Akira?"

Akira doesn't speak for a while. "You have a child, Ginger," he says, finally.

"I do." Although she can imagine where he is headed, she'll not put words in his mouth. As with the waltz, she will follow his lead.

"It's important to a man," he says.

"You'd like a child."

"I would not have married my wife if I'd known she would be unable to bear me children."

"That's a terrible thing to say."

"Is it? Maybe in America it is an unpopular notion. Here, perhaps, a man's desire for a child is something people still understand."

"I understand it," Ginger says. "It just seems cruel to me that you would want to abandon your wife because she can't bring a child into the world for you. She would change things herself if she could, wouldn't she?"

"Of course. But you misunderstand me—I'm not abandoning my wife."

"You said you'd have married differently had you known."

"That's not the same thing as abandonment."

"I see." Somehow the conversation, while enlightening, doesn't make Ginger feel any better than she did before she called a halt to their lovemaking. Now she feels bad in a different way—she sees that her relationship with Akira truly holds no promise. Not only does her religious tradition preclude her from marrying a divorced man, this man does not even intend to divorce his wife.

"Does Megumi have lovers?"

"That's her business." Akira sits up and reaches for his yukata. "But, no, I don't think she does. My wife has lost interest in sex, at least with me. That is acknowledged between us."

"Did you love her when you married her?"

"It was an arranged marriage. I thought I would come to love her."

"Does she love you?"

"I don't know. Look, we've got a busy day ahead of us. Lots of driving again. I need to get some sleep." His bare feet cross the mat, the yukata a column swaying above them. "There's a foam pillow on the top shelf of the closet if you want one," he says, sliding the door closed after him.

Ginger lies awake for a long time, until the moon has moved past her windows.

TEN

Ocha

From the passage comes a rustling, and then Yuki's cry. "Oniru-san! Oniru-san!"

Rolling from her futon, Ginger gains her wobbly legs and slides the door open.

"*Denwa*," Yuki says, and holds her hand up next to her cheek, her thumb and little finger extended. Ginger is wanted on the telephone. Suddenly aware of her nakedness, Ginger throws on her yukata and in bare feet runs down the stairs to reception. The telephone, handset off the hook, sits on a low bookcase. Ginger picks up the handset.

"Ginger, your sister called."

"Sakiko? What time is it?"

"Seven."

Ginger is trying to remember where she is.

"Your sister said it's emergency. Police have your daughter."

"Bernie?"

"*Hai*. Your sister didn't say what happen. She wants you to call home."

"I can't call home. How could I call home?"

"Try to call from ryokan, then come back to Osaka. Ask Akira-san to bring you."

"How will I call home?" Ginger notices the fan on the high ceiling of the reception area, the fan spinning around and around. Already the morning air is hot with the dragon's breath. Maybe the dragon could save her from reality, blowing her out into the sea, away from her life.

"Akira-san will help you."

"But how did you find me, Sakiko?" The question, while relevant to Ginger, she asks primarily as a means to avoid thinking about Bernie.

"When your sister called, I phoned Akira-san's house. I asked Megumi-san if she know where her husband is. She didn't know," Sakiko goes on, "but she called me back few minutes later. She checked her husband's bank statements. She found names of some ryokan where he went. I called three, and then I found you."

"Oh, my God." Ginger closes her eyes and begins to sway. Yuki appears at her side, pulling up a chair for her. Ginger's ears are ringing, the outside world closing off to her, but Sakiko is trying to tell her something.

"Your sister called early in morning and said Bernie is in trouble. Nothing more."

"Is Bernie—"

"I'm sorry. I have no more to tell you." She hesitates, and adds, "I am sure things will be all right." Then she hangs up.

Yuki leads Ginger to the steps, which Ginger can only crawl up. Akira meets her at the top of the flight.

"What's going on?" He rubs his face and runs his hands through his tangled hair.

"I don't know. I need to get home. I need to get back to Osaka. I must make plans."

"Can you take care of things from here?" Akira asks.

"How soon can we leave?" Ginger responds.

"I'll book the ferry for you. Let me help you call your home."

They go back downstairs, and Akira dials the numbers Ginger gives him. There's no answer at Ginger's house or at Reggie's house. Reggie's cell phone, like the house phones, offers only a recording. Even Ginger's own cell phone, which Ginger is letting Bernie use this month, is set to automatic answering. Ginger leaves messages everywhere.

"I'll call the ferry," Akira says, "then we can go."

"You aren't going to take me back to Osaka?"

"I want to spend some time today in Kobe, to see those prints I told you about. The ferry will be faster.

You'll be back in Osaka in no time. It will be much longer if we drive."

Yuki serves Ginger's breakfast on the low table in Ginger's room—miso soup, soft-boiled egg, grilled fish, rice, seaweed. All Ginger can do is drink some *ocha*. Tea.

Bag in hand, Ginger is in the foyer, trying to settle her account with the ryokan manager, but the woman's English is poor and Ginger can't make herself understood. Akira arrives from his room and speaks to the manager.

"Ginger, the bill is taken care of."

"Taken care of?"

"It's settled. Let's go."

"I know what *taken care of* means, but what *I* mean is that I want to pay my share. How many yen was my room?"

"Ryokan charges are complicated. We can talk about it later." Akira picks up his case and walks out the door.

Whether Ginger's tears come from rage or fear isn't clear, but she suppresses them and makes her way to the car. She climbs in and shuts the door, settling her bag on her lap.

"What time is the ferry?"

"Nine forty-five."

"And when will I be in Osaka?"

"The trip is only ninety minutes."

It will be nearly midnight in Nether Gorge by the time Ginger reaches the Murakamis' house.

"I did try to get you on the catamaran but had no luck."

"What do you mean?"

"The high-speed ferry to and from Kansai Airport." Akira lights a cigarette. "It would be half the time," he says, dropping his lighter back into his shirt pocket, "but it's full of tourists coming to and from the island. So I got you a space on the car ferry. You'll get back faster than if we drove straight there."

"But I don't have a car!"

"That's okay. You don't need one on the ferry." Akira rolls a cigarette between his fingers. "What did your sister say about your daughter?"

"Sakiko said nothing."

If Akira finds Ginger's remark ambiguous, he turns a blind eye to any curiosity he may have. In silence they drive to Tsuna Town and the dock. Ginger, on some level of consciousness, is aware of the high filaments of clouds, crocheted strands of silky yarn.

Ginger yanks open her door as Akira pulls to a stop. He puts the car in park, sets the brake, and opens his own door. Ginger is halfway to the water before she realizes she needs him in order to pick up her ticket. She stops dead and waits for him.

"Ginger, you seem angry with me," Akira says, leading her to the ticket line. "I'm trying to help you."

"Help me?" Her voice startles even her; it sounds like the wailing of an ambulance.

"Calm down. You'll make yourself sick."

"Just how do you think you're helping me?"

"I've done everything to expedite your return to the mainland. Called about the ferry, helped you place your calls."

"I need something more than that," Ginger shouts, and now the other people in line are paying attention to the arguing couple.

"What? What do you need?" Akira's voice, unlike Ginger's, is restrained.

Ginger, normally in control of her emotions in public, uses her voice as a weapon for her anger, admonishing Akira and justifying herself.

"You have no children, and practically no family, and from what I can see you pay no attention to your wife. You take woman after woman away to ryokans. How would you know how it feels to be this far from your loved ones?"

"Wait a minute. What's this about taking women to ryokan?"

"Your wife helped Sakiko find us."

"I thought she might have."

"You've been here before."

"I've been lots of places before. But you've got the women part wrong."

"Yeah?"

Akira pays for the ferry ticket. Without looking back, Ginger grabs it from the cashier and boards the ferry.

In the cabin, Ginger walks past the vending machines, then backs up and scrutinizes them. They're full of sugary soft drinks, as well as sweetened iced coffees, sports drinks, bottled water, tea, and beer. Ginger would like a Diet Coke, but there are no diet sodas in the machines. She buys a bottle of cold tea, and it tastes like pure tannin. Once they are underway, Ginger goes back out on deck and stands next to the railing, next to the choppy water. Awaji Island is receding over the stern of the boat. Ginger studies the seascape, observing both oil slicks passing beneath the ferry and dirty gulls dropping into the bay for their slithery fish dinners.

The day is already hot, and Ginger forgot to pack her hat for the trip to the island. She sets her tote next to her feet, at the edge of the railing. A tall man comes and stands alongside her, walks away, then returns to stand closer. She moves to starboard and looks towards the equator. She has never been to the other side of that imaginary line. The man doesn't follow Ginger.

Ginger tries to find some shade on deck, and, seeing none, heads back inside to the air conditioning. She takes off her shoes and enters the carpeted family area. A few children are playing with a large ball, their parents seated on the floor along the perimeter of the room. Ginger sits with her back to the wall, leans against it, and closes her eyes.

Ginger is filled with remorse—remorse for coming to Japan when she has a daughter at home, remorse for encouraging whatever relationship she and Akira had, remorse for making the trip to Awaji. She is ashamed of not latching her door and of letting Akira into her bed. She wishes it had only been a dream, but she's sure it was real. And perversely, Ginger is remorseful about not completing the act of love. If she's going to be punished for her behavior with Akira by having something horrible happen to her daughter, she might as well have enjoyed it.

Ginger is already in a state of grief, grief not just for the loss she anticipates she'll find when she gets in touch with her sister, but grief for being let down by a man for whom she had come to feel admiration and affection. She wants to be free from the restrictions of her background, free to handle this situation in whatever direction it takes, yet she knows that a faith tradition performs the social function of setting boundaries for human behavior. It has crossed her mind that her religion may have infantilized her, keeping her from making decisions on her own, but within what framework can a person make decisions if the person possesses no values? Don't mainstream religions support, even impose, sets of values, ones that have been tested by time? There's nothing wrong with having something outside yourself to answer to. Ginger has demanded structure and rules. Now she doesn't want them to apply to her.

Even in the cooler air Ginger is sweaty. A glance at her watch tells her the ferry is thirty minutes from port.

She has pains in her stomach. Perhaps she has finally diseased herself with raw fish, Reggie having been right all along—sushi is dangerous. The parasites in raw fish could be having their way with Ginger. Or she could be seasick. Or sick with fear.

With twenty minutes to go, outside the skies are growing gray. From Ginger's slumped position on the floor, it seems Akira is among the passengers; all the middle-aged men look alike. The cramps in her abdomen are intensifying, and suddenly she's desperate to find the restroom. She tries to stand just as the ferry heaves with the seas, and she falls onto a young woman sitting nearby with a baby in her arms. Ginger apologizes in English, having forgotten the most rudimentary Japanese she learned. The woman nods and looks away. Ginger's shoes are where she left them, and with great labor she tugs them on and stumbles down the hall.

At first she turns in the wrong direction, and vomit is in her throat as she finally pushes open the ladies' room door. The Japanese toilet, long and flush with the floor, is the image of a toothless mouth. Ginger retches up the morning's *ocha*, the acid burning her throat, and with her arm wipes away the brownish liquid that drips from her nose. She locks the stall door, steps out of her slacks and panties, and straddles the toilet, squatting over it. Japanese toilets can serve several functions at once—from this spot Ginger can even throw up. Her legs tremble and ache but she dares not move.

The air pressure changes as someone opens the restroom door, followed by the door's quick swoosh as that someone hurries out. She may have gone for help; she may have recoiled from the stench. Ginger cleans herself and dresses, leaves the stall, and lies next to the sink on the cool, tiled floor. She looks once more at her watch. The ferry will dock in five minutes.

Ginger had fainted in the pew at Steve's funeral. Bernie was sitting next to her, in Reggie's lap. Ginger's head made such a thunk when she fell forward that the overwhelmed Irish-immigrant priest had cried out, "Holy Mother of God, pray for the young widow!" Ginger had laughed when Reggie told her this story after the funeral Mass, but in the limousine on their way to the cemetery Ginger lost consciousness again after throwing up on her new, black, wool crepe dress. Reggie'd pulled smelling salts from her purse, opened a package, and stuck the salts up Ginger's nose, one in each nostril. Every time Ginger sees a tampon she thinks of those smelling salts and inexplicably gets a whiff of ammonium carbonate.

Hiro's face looks like a green Greek olive, pit in, a darkish oval, the ferry's unforgiving ceiling lights behind him. He is beautiful as he comes in and out of Ginger's focus. His soft voice says, "Jinja, Jinja, wake up," and his soothing pressure on her wrist is a relief for her, but the brightness of the lights hurts her eyes. Sakiko stands behind him, crowded into the women's room with strangers. Medics lift Ginger onto a stretcher. Sakiko tells Ginger that she'll be okay, that they're going to the hospital and then home. As Ginger is carried into the sunlight and heat, she touches the *mala* wrapped around her fingers. She had found the Buddhist prayer beads on the restroom sink. The *mala* is strung with clear crystals, and Ginger clings to it, whispering the Five Glorious Mysteries, prayers of the Catholic rosary, as she's transported to the hospital. The smooth spheres are a succor; the rhythm of repetition calms her. Saying the rosary may help to compensate for Ginger's having missed Mass two Sundays in a row, but soon the rhythm of her prayers, together with her regained consciousness, makes her think of music, and then of Akira, and finally of sex, and that brings back her nausea. At last a hand reaches in and tenders Ginger salt tablets, the kind athletes take after a workout. Another hand brushes them away and applies a tourniquet, searching for a vein. The rehydrating intravenous line begins its work.

ELEVEN

Umeshu

Ginger can see the sky again. Bernie is safe. Arrested, but safe.

"Where were you?" Reggie asks.

"At Awaji. On Awaji."

"Awaji?" Her voice has an edgy sound.

"An island not far from here."

"A tropical island?"

"Subtropical, supratropical. Reggie, listen, I'm sorry. I should have been there for Bernie. But tell me what happened."

"Joyriding, underage drinking, vandalism." Reggie emphasizes each offense, pausing between them.

"And no one was hurt?"

"Thank God, no."

"I'll see about getting a flight out tonight. Is Bernie in jail?"

"It would be juvenile detention," Reggie corrects her, "but no, she's here at home. She's been assigned a case worker from intake. And don't bother coming home early. Stay out your appointment. There's nothing you can do. You'll be home by the time Bernie has her date with Mother Justice." Reggie laughs. "So, what were you doing on a supertropical island?"

"*Supra*tropical, I said. And I'm not sure what I was doing there."

"What kind of an island is that? And how can you not be sure?"

"It's complex."

"I can handle complexities, Virginia Marie, even subtleties."

"*Mary Regine*, I said I'm sorry."

"I know. I shouldn't be snappy with you. God knows you've tried to bring your daughter up properly. It's just been a long night. And I don't want to be frozen out of *Ginger Does Japan*. Who's the guy? Your last e-mails have been evasive. Something's up."

"I'll explain when I get home. But let me understand—Bernie's safe and sound?"

"As safe and sound as can be expected, with a pissed-off aunt, a globe-trotting mother, and a rap sheet."

Reggie offers the essentials of the situation, but the phone line has a ship-to-shore delay on it, and the sisters end up talking over one another.

Finally Ginger says, "Let me talk to Bernie. And thanks for everything you're doing, Reg."

"You're welcome. I'll go wake her up. We were asleep when you called, but don't worry about that. What you do need to worry about is that Bernie wonders where you've been—*unavailable* I told her, because that was the truth. But she asked a lot of questions about how you could be unavailable for such a long stretch of time, through your night. Be aware that she wondered, when she was banging dishes around in my kitchen, how you can expect her to behave if you don't."

After a five-dollar interval, Bernie picks up the phone on an extension. "Hi, Mom."

Reggie clicks off.

"Hi, sweetie."

"Where were you, Mom?"

Ginger turns a deaf ear to the past tense of her daughter's question. "I'm in Osaka, at Hiro and Sakiko's."

"We couldn't find you." Her voice carries a certain level of concern.

"I know. I'm here now. Tell me what happened."

"We had a party."

"You and your new Confederate friends?"

"No, my regular friends from St. Mary's. You always think so poorly of the public school kids, Mom. The parochial school kids are just as bad."

"Apparently. Tell me what happened."

"It started out so well." Bernie sounds almost enthusiastic. "I never, ever thought it would get out of hand."

"What do you mean?"

"Francie Wilson had a sleep-over—girls only, not like her last one, you know, the one you wouldn't let me go to? Anyway, she had a sleep-over while her parents were away for the weekend," Bernie says quickly. The days of Ouija boards and contact lenses dropped down the sink are gone; gone are the days too of girls staying up all night talking *about* boys, rather than talking *to* them. Today's kids have co-ed slumber parties, explaining to their parents that they're preparing for college and life in co-ed dorms. Their parents, caught between doing what they think is right and wanting their kids to be popular, or at least not stuck in the mud, allow them to attend these sleepovers. What parents like Ginger can't figure out is what actually goes on at them. But this one, fortunately, was single-sex.

"And then what, Bernie?"

"Uh, it got kind of crazy, Mom. Some boys dropped in."

"Dropped in?"

"They sort of crashed the party, but it wasn't their fault."

Did someone hold a gun to their heads? Ginger thinks, but she keeps her sarcasm to herself.

"Aunt Reggie says there was drinking at the party."

"Yeah, well, we opened up the Wilsons' wine cellar. They have one of those big things that looks like a giant refrigerator. It's so cool."

"Bernie, we've talked about this before. You're not supposed to be drinking. It's illegal and dangerous, regardless what your friends say."

"You drink."

"Go on with your story."

"It was okay—we cut the wine with spritzer and juice. Francie's parents have a juicer, and we made our own mixes."

"Bernie! Get to the point. What happened when the boys arrived?"

"They'd had a few beers by the time they got there, and they brought more with them to share."

"And?" *Dear God, please let them not have paired off into the bedrooms.*

"The guys trashed the house. Threw the crystal in the fireplace, took an antique lamp to the TV, and did a bunch of annoying guy things," Bernie goes on. "We couldn't control them, Mom," she adds, "and Francie got hysterical."

"Aunt Reggie said something about joyriding."

"We didn't think of it like that. After the boys left, Francie drank a lot. She said she wanted to pass out." Ginger wouldn't be able to say she blames her, but she's quiet, while Bernie continues. "Later on—yesterday I guess that was—I've kind of lost track of time—the other girls and I took Mrs. Wilson's car to go have our nails done. She's got that cool sporty Mercedes. We wanted to get those—"

"And the cops picked you up?"

"—little dragonflies on our nails." Bernie takes a breath and addresses her mother's question after Ginger repeats it. "Yeah, the cops picked us up. It was daytime, so I don't know why we got pulled over. Something about a lane change, I guess."

"Who was driving?"

"Me. But the alcohol had worn off by this time—it was after lunch that we had our appointments—so I wasn't charged with driving under the influence. And Aunt Reggie says some of the charges might not stick."

She was arrested while Ginger was lying on her futon, Akira in her arms.

"I'm disappointed in you, Bernie. We've talked about all this. You've got to be careful, especially with a group of kids."

"I know." And then she turns the question around to Ginger, and again in her voice is concern for her mother. "Are you being careful, Mom?"

"Like everyone else, sometimes I'm better than at other times." Ginger scratches a mosquito bite on her leg. "Aunt Reggie said you met the intake officer. Do you have a court date?"

"No, but I might have to go before a jury of my peers. Do you think they'll be harder on me than adults would be?"

"I can't imagine."

"The Wilsons want restitution for wrecking their house. Luckily nothing happened to the car. I bet they're feeling stupid for leaving Francie home alone while they went to New York for the weekend."

The Wilsons have never impressed Ginger as mental giants. "You have money from babysitting and selling the tie-dyed T-shirts. You can step up production and use some of your savings."

"Yeah."

"Do you want me to come home?"

"No. What do you have, one week left? We'll be fine. Aunt Reggie is working with the other parents on our contribution."

"I'm sure she has everything under control." Ginger is going to owe Reggie big-time. But maybe Ginger's presence isn't actually necessary twenty-four hours a day, seven days a week, even when things go wrong. "Bernie, we'll need to discuss this more when I get home. Obviously, there'll be public consequences for what you've done. I'll give some thought to what household measures we'll take."

"Ah, geez, Mom," is the girl's response, and then, after a moment, "I'm sorry."

"We all do dumb things. What's important is to learn from them."

"I wish you were here."

"You sure I shouldn't come home?"

"No, you have a life, too. You're entitled to have some fun. But what were you doing? Where were you?"

"On a teacher outing. No big deal. Listen, thank Aunt Reggie again for me."

"I will."

Ginger has something else on her mind but her usual fluidity with language is failing her. "Uh, Bernie, I don't know how to put this, but you don't need to see a doctor, do you?"

"Not an issue, Mom. I'm not going to mess up my life like that."

"Sure?"

"No funny stuff in the sleeping bags, if that makes you feel better."

"I'm not feeling good about not being there for you. I should have been."

"You can't stay home waiting for when I'll need you."

"You're right."

"Mom, when I asked you where you'd been, I didn't mean you should have been only at the Murakamis' house. I was just wondering if you'd been some place interesting."

"I *was* some place interesting, but I didn't enjoy it much, at least once I found out you were in trouble."

"Do you think I could go with you next time you travel?"

"Possibly—"

"Maybe Aunt Reggie could go too, you know, the way we all used to go places together. Aunt Reggie can be fun, even if she's kind of intense."

"I know she can be fun. Let's think about it and then plan something when I get back. If Aunt Reggie's still speaking to us. Is she terribly put out?"

"She acts like it, but I think she likes having a legal issue to mess around with. Something more exciting than taxes, if you know what I mean. Hey, I love you and can't wait to see you and hear all about your trip. Have fun and take care of yourself and don't worry about me. I'm going to be in the company of only my chemistry books until you get home."

"Good idea." Ginger will drop Reggie an e-mail to say Bernie shouldn't leave the house other than to go to school.

"I know I messed up and I'll work to straighten this out. I still want to have an acting career, and I know I need to take my responsibilities seriously for that to work. I was just wondering—"

"What?"

"I was wondering if the next time you go out for sushi, after you come home that is, if I could go with you and try the raw fish. I'm tired of always eating California roll with fake crabmeat."

"Okay."

"Don't you think I'm old enough to have the fatty tuna?" Bernie hasn't heard her mother. "I know it's good because of the look you get on your face when you eat it. I can even be the designated driver if you want to have a few beers."

"Bernie, you're not going to be driving for a long time, but we can eat sushi together. Eating raw fish is more problematic for old people, so I'll appreciate the years I have left to enjoy it with you." As if Ginger has any intention of giving up eating raw fish in ten, twenty, or even thirty years.

"I love you, Mom."

"I love you, too, sweetie. I'm glad you're okay."

Ginger hangs up and finds Sakiko in the kitchen, flipping through her latest issue of *Kateigaho*. Sakiko's focused on an ad for Bally bags. Ginger tells her Bernie is fine.

"Ginger, I don't want to say anything until you are sure Bernie is okay. Our principal called earlier today. He left message. He wants to see you first thing tomorrow morning."

"Oh, Sakiko, will you ever have another American guest?"

"Of course, Ginger, why not?"

"I've been so much trouble, keeping you and Hiro up half the night, and now you've spent your day at the dock and hospital. I'm sure you have better things to do."

"It's no problem, Ginger. We are glad you have chance to do here what you don't do at home. I'm sorry Awaji trip ended badly."

Mai enters the kitchen, and Sakiko speaks in Japanese to her.

"I'm happy to know that your daughter is okay, Ginger-san."

"Thank you, Mai."

"Mai, Ginger-san and I will share *umeshu* now. Would you like some?"

"*Kekko desu*. I have test tomorrow. Excuse me." Mai takes a glass of water from the pitcher in the refrigerator and leaves the room.

"Umeshu?"

"You will love my plum wine."

"Maybe if I'd let Bernie drink wine with me she wouldn't be chugging it at parties."

"No way to tell what children do." Sakiko pulls a fat bottle and two glasses from a cupboard. Now would be a good time for Ginger to tell Sakiko about Mai and her friend among the pillows.

"I just don't ordinarily behave like this, Sakiko. The wildest thing I ever did was to date a Baptist."

"Where did you meet your husband?"

"At church, after I broke up with the Baptist. I was working on my master's degree. Steve took up the collection at the church near campus and grinned at me each Sunday when I tossed in my fifty cents."

"You introduced yourself to your husband?"

"How did you know?" Is Ginger's life written on her forehead? "The problem is that sometimes I'm not sure what's right and what's wrong."

"Hai."

"But in this case, in my case, I think I do know." The wine is syrupy; the alcohol has made Ginger sweat, even though the air conditioner is cooling the kitchen.

"You are smart lady."

"Not smart enough. What I mean is, even in a culture as different from mine as yours, a woman doesn't marry a man so he can have carnal knowledge of another woman."

"Eh?"

"I'm stepping into Megumi's territory. Into something that belongs to Megumi."

"You do not know what Megumi-san wants of marriage."

"Do you know?"

"Nobody knows but Megumi-san and maybe her husband."

"What do you want of marriage, Sakiko?"

"I want husband to support me. Money and emotion. He is good with money but not always good with emotion."

"Do you ever think about other men?"

"You kidding me? Of course! But only think, so far."

"A special person?"

"Maybe. More plum wine, Ginger?"

"I'm just so angry with Akira for leaving me at the ferry." She holds her glass out for more.

"I think he did right thing. Get you here faster."

"But why didn't he come with me? He didn't have to go to Kobe. That was optional."

"Maybe he promised someone he is going to Kobe. Maybe shop owner."

Ginger can understand commitments. She herself is aggrieved when people cancel engagements on her, when they let her down. She is particularly hard on herself when she has let someone else down.

"Akira's the wrong religion, anyway," Ginger says.

"What do you say?"

"Did I say something? Never mind, I was just thinking out loud."

"Your daughter is almost grown up. Soon she will be on her own. You can travel and meet new people. Fall in love. Marry again."

"One thing today has shown me is that Bernie will be all right even if I'm not there every moment. I feel both good and bad about that. I'm not essential to her life, which makes me feel bad, but it's good to think of having a life of my own again. And of her having a life of her own."

"I should think that way too. You help me think about my daughter, Ginger. Mai grow up too. Not always need me."

234 Mary Claire Mahaney

"We're in the same boat."

"You are in love with Akira-san?"

"I'm afraid I might be. I should just enjoy that feeling, shouldn't I?"

Sakiko nods.

"I just wish I knew where I was headed. I'd like some excitement, Sakiko, but I also want to feel secure."

"Maybe person cannot have excitement and be secure at same time."

"I don't want to be vulnerable," Ginger says, finishing her drink, "but you could be right. Yes, you *are* right. In fact, not knowing the future is what makes life exciting."

Sakiko nods and stands up. "Ginger, I must go to my husband. He has no attention from me today. He likes me to be with him." She's quiet for a moment. "You know, Japanese man is very good at keeping different parts of life—how do you say—"

"Separate? *Compartmentalizing*, we call it. It's not a trait reserved for Japanese men."

Sakiko picks up her magazine. "It must be hard to be only parent for your daughter."

"It is hard, and it's hard to be a widow. I need human affection. And I like men."

"And men like you."

"Why do you say that?"

"You are attractive."

"Really?"

"More than you know."

"I doubt Akira is thinking that now."

Sakiko laughs. "Sorry, Ginger, but sometime you are funny and don't know it. You will find someone."

"You know, I did go out with a nice, older man whom I've thought of since I've been here. His children were grown, he was widowed himself, and he was Catholic and liked opera. I thought we might have a future together."

"What happen to him?"

"The last date we had was for a sitar recital at the Indian embassy. We had discovered we both were passionate about the sitar, so for three hours we sat on the floor at the embassy, cross-legged, listening to Indian music."

"Bad to sit on floor for that long for music."

"We overdid it a bit. Americans aren't used to sitting on the floor for hours. When the performance was over, my friend couldn't stand up. He had to crawl out of the room."

"You're joking."

"I'm not. It was humiliating for him."

"Then what?"

"The embassy called the house doctor, who massaged my friend's legs until he could straighten them out. I drove us to his house in his car and called a cab for myself. I never heard from him after that."

"Long time ago?"

"Eight years. He could be dead by now."

"You have regret about trip to Awaji?"

Ginger doesn't answer, and Sakiko finds a bag of sweet, soy-sauced crackers among her pots and pans. She opens the package and sets it in front of Ginger. "In case you need something to eat while I'm with my husband. To be honest, my husband, he is excited. Having you here excites him. He wants me."

"Hurry to him, then! I'll stay down here."

"Thank you, Ginger-san."

One might think by coming halfway around the world Ginger would have escaped her cultural and religious biases, but being here and meeting Akira has only brought them into sharper focus. It's not possible to escape one's life. Ginger's upbringing will forever be a part of her. As Dr. Ledsmar says in *Theron Ware*, "There's no bottom to the Catholic Church. Everything that's in, stays in."

Monday, July 17

With the Akira episode behind me, I summoned up my nerve tonight and called Ken McMillan. There was no answer at his home, and the machine gave me a message in Japanese. I wasn't sure it was his voice, so I hung up. Then I asked Sakiko to call his number and listen to the message. We'd agreed, she and I, that she would hand me the phone if she heard either his name or number on the recording. One would think with all that preparation I might have said something intelligent into the phone, yet when I finally spoke I could merely make some garbled sounds and then, warmed up, I went on ad nauseam about being in Osaka and hoping to get together. Sakiko was scribbling out a note with my name on it so I'd remember to say who I was, but I couldn't focus on it and hung up without leaving my name. I did think, however, to leave the Murakamis' phone number. I'll be surprised if Ken calls back.

Hiro has some great CDs sitting around my room—Beatles' music, Puccini's *The Girl of the Golden West*, the Irish Tenors. The last of these is still in its cellophane. "Danny Boy" is on that album, twice. I'd like to listen to Hiro's music, but I hate to bother him with showing me how to use his sound system. It's something that isn't essential to my well-being. I'm keeping Sakiko and him busy as it is.

At dinner tonight I spilled red wine on Sakiko's white tablecloth. Sakiko looked as if she were going to cry. "This soil-release fabric does not always work," she said. I apologized and offered to put the tablecloth in the washer, even to buy her a new tablecloth, but she handed it to Mai with paragraphs' worth of oral instructions on how to treat the stain. Mai never came back to dinner. And I've been so good—putting coasters under everything the way I do at home, even holding my glass instead of setting it down if I can't find a coaster.

As for the issue of Mai (and love among the pillows), I've given it a lot of thought since Friday night and have decided not to mention it to Sakiko. After all, where's the harm in a lesbian relationship? No one is going to get pregnant; no one is going to get a disease. In terms of Bernie, for instance, would I want to know if she were in a homosexual relationship? I would want to know about it only if Bernie wanted me to know, and I wouldn't want to be told about it by a houseguest. It's possible Sakiko already knows about Mai and her friend.

My week is going to be busy. The principal has asked for my help with several last-minute projects. (That's all he wanted me for last night—and I was so nervous about seeing him.) I worked with the editor of the school web site; she needs at least one page of the site to be in English, so I corrected some copy for her. Also, the school is expanding its English program—more and more elementary schools are offering English instruction, so the high schools will be offering higher level English, which means they'll be hiring more English teachers. The assistant principal asked me to look over some ads they want to place in American educational bulletins. He wondered if I might like to teach here. I told him I'd have to give it some thought. The thought scares me. Live in Japan? I'm having enough trouble just visiting.

Tomorrow I'll meet with the English club after school and review the lists of English texts that Mrs. Kitajima drew up—literary works she thinks may help the students move beyond simple grammar and diction. She appears to have had a change of heart, or mind. The PTA has money, she said, to spend on paperback copies for the classroom. She wants me to recommend movies that the students can see along with their reading. *The Age of Innocence* comes to mind.

Mrs. K. asked about the journals that I have my students keep. On a whim, I spoke of the students' *journalizing*—it has a self-referential, classy sort of sound to it, compared to the down-talk of that insidious *journaling*. I've decided to use *journalizing* when I go back to Confederate. It should shake up the other English teachers. I've been thinking a lot about Confederate lately, wondering how long I'll teach there. I've never dreamed of doing anything other than teach, until this trip, that is, but lately I've been considering other options. I'm re-energized about the partnership and would like to see it succeed (it may be the only good thing to come of this trip), but I'm thinking next year might be my last at Confederate. That would allow me free time for Bernie's senior year—I could do some substitute teaching on my own schedule—and then I could do what I've never done as much as I would like: travel. I could have great stretches of time away from Nether Gorge.

I had an e-mail from Reggie. Late last night I'd sent her the most cursory of info on Akira—that he's a music teacher, that he likes literature, that he's handsome. This morning she asked if I'm *using* him to win the partnership. Surely people here aren't thinking that! Surely Akira isn't thinking—

Sakiko called me as I was writing. Ken was on the phone. He recognized my voice. I don't suppose he gets many phone calls from English speakers. He runs a coffee shop in a close-by suburb and wants me to meet him there Wednesday evening. Sakiko offered to drive me. He sounded the same. After all these years!

Tuesday, July 18
Dear Bernie,

Today the sky was white at the horizon, pale blue overhead, as if a painter had laid cerulean blue at the top of her paper, then thinned her watercolor paint with water, sweeping it out farther and farther to the bottom, with each brush stroke drawing up less and less pigment and more and more water. The sky reminded me of you because of how much you like to wear blue and how good it looks on you. The air wasn't as stifling today as it has been, but I've got my air conditioner on here in my room nevertheless. The outside air is by no means cool, even though the sun has set.

Bernie, I don't want to belabor the things we talked about on Sunday—about your responsibilities, about how bad I feel I wasn't home for you, and about the consequences of your actions. Therefore I won't say anything more about it, for the moment. We both need time to think, to process all that has happened.

My work here veers from the intensity of meetings with school staff to hours of idleness in which I think and read and write. I'm glad I brought my little library of reading material. It's not like traveling in the States, where, if I run out of unread books, I can find a bookstore and buy a book. Of course I can find bookstores in Japan; it's just hard to find anything in them that I would be able to read.

I know you get tired of my preaching about English usage, Bernie, but here people haven't heard my sermons, and I'm enjoying explaining usage to everyone who asks. I've been able to express myself on issues like bring and take, about raising chickens but rearing children, about how unpleasant the word author is used as a verb. I even got into a spirited discussion with one of the English teachers about the way American teens say "I'm fine," when they mean "No thank you." I told the teacher how when you and your friends use the "I'm fine" expression, I always say I haven't asked them how they are, I've asked them if they want more to eat, or whatever. What I learned is that Kekko desu, which means No thank you, is literal for I'm fine. That was humbling to hear, and so I've decided to change my tune about I'm fine. You may want to let your friends know that your mom is coming home a changed woman.

You're never going to believe this, but after all these years I have a new love in my life—writing! Yesterday I started on the third volume of my Japan journal. Two things I'm finding most enjoyable: writing down the details, details that will jog my memory and allow me to relive my experiences when I read my diary years from now; and thinking on the page. Writing helps me follow my thoughts to their (sometimes absurd) conclusions. I don't know that I'll get any smarter by keeping a journal, but surely I won't lose ground.

What would you say if I quit teaching after this coming year? Then I could help you with your college applications. Have you given any thought to schools you want to visit? We'll need to do that this year. I'm thinking you'll want to look in California or New York, some place with an acting industry. You're thinking film over stage, aren't you? I wish you'd stay on the East Coast, because it's closer to home, but I can cope with it if you fall in love with a school out West. I can barely stand to think of your going away from me, Bernie, but I want you to follow your dream.

One last thing: I've been reminded here that you don't ever know a people until you know their language, or at least about their language. For example, Sakiko doesn't call her husband by his name, not to me anyway. She always refers to him as "my husband." I wonder what that says about the relationship between husband and wife. Also between parents and children—to me she calls Mai "my daughter," never "Mai." What effect do you think language has on relationships, and what effect do relationships have on language?

Bernie, I'll be home before you get this, but that's okay. I'll be even happier to see you than this letter will!

Love,
Mom

From: Ginger O'Neill (<u>sushilover@mailforall.com</u>)
To: Reggie Conway, Esq. (<u>taxlit@anonymail.com</u>)
Subject: Tuesday update

Reg,

A few minutes ago I got an e-mail from a woman I met on the train when I arrived. She was the woman I told you about, the one in the kimono, the one who helped me find my way to Namba. I had given her my business card, and I told her if she was ever in our area she should look me up. She has looked me up, already. She's a production assistant at a Kansai television station, and she mentioned me to her boss. They've asked me to be on a show the day after tomorrow. They want me to demonstrate how to prepare an American barbecue. It's part of a series on foreign customs. The host of the show is a local celebrity. He used to be a hair stylist for the station and worked his way onto the sound stage, Sakiko tells me.

I know what you're thinking, Reg—that I can't cook to save my life, but this sounds like a good opportunity to try something different. It's not that I can't cook, or couldn't if I tried, you know. Marine Day, the day of the show, is a national holiday. We won't have school that day. The kimono woman, Junko-san, apologized for the short notice (I had the feeling some other programming had fallen through) and said she hopes this will work out because she'd like to see me again. I've already told Sakiko about it, and she's so excited she's called at least four of her friends. She said she'd get the ingredients for me. I'm going to ask if Sakiko can be on the show as well.

Do you remember the cookout Helen had last summer? She sat a chicken on top of a beer can, and the meat was terrific—so tender, so juicy. That's what I'm going to fix. I've already found a recipe for it on the Internet. We'll also have a green salad and potato salad and corn bread and chocolate cake.

It's hard to believe, but I'm not getting fat. I eat everything put in front of me, but my clothes aren't tight. The food here isn't as rich as ours, and the portions are smaller. What a lark it would be to live here!

I'm sorry to hear Jeff's a member of the Unification Church, although I thought Moonies were more repressed than he appears to be. Sexually repressed, I mean. You've dropped him, I presume, his beliefs surely getting in the way of your professed agnosticism or atheism or whatever it is.

I meant to mention I saw that piece in the *Post* today, Walk the Walk as big as life on the front page of the Metro section. He's shooting off his mouth, you know, saying he has the partnership in his pocket. I haven't misled him. He can say whatever he wants. Whether we get this school is out of his control.

Must quit. Bedtime for Ginger. Oh, I almost forgot. I see Ken tomorrow night. Wish me luck.

Ginger

Wednesday, July 19

Ken hasn't changed a bit.

He had half a dozen staff working during the hour and a half I was at his shop, and each of them was hard at it every moment. The coffee shop is open from six in the morning until midnight seven days a week; Ken says he spends at least twelve hours a day there. He took me on a tour behind the scenes. It was more orderly in the back rooms than I would have thought, given the near-chaos out front. Maybe *chaos* isn't the best of words—*frenetic* would better describe it, organized, but intense, brisk. Not a place I would go to settle down with a book.

That wasn't technically true two paragraphs above when I wrote that Ken hasn't changed. He has aged, as have we all, and he has grown slightly portly. He still has his charm, a quality that drew me to him in the first place twenty-five years ago. I could tell from the way he looked at me, the way he leaned forward as we sat at the table and talked, that he is still fond of me. (And I could picture the two of us in the grass once more, God help me!) He said he'd never thought he'd see me again. It was clear I was making him happy just being there. He has never married, never found the right woman, he said. He'd heard I was married but hadn't heard I was widowed. His reaction to the latter seemed mixed. Initially a smile appeared on his face, then his cheeks and neck turned red. He said only, "I wish I had known."

At the beginning of our visit, Ken told me he's committed to living in Japan and sees no future for himself in America. He never fit in back in the States, he said, his mother's Japanese influence on him too great to allow him to overlook the differences between the cultures. He said he struggles to fit in here, too, but that he likes the customs and the pace. He struck me as a man without a country, and that was something I'd not considered before—the fate of people whose parents are from different backgrounds and who are brought up living around the world. People like Ken fit in nowhere. Some people would like that sort of rootless way of life; I don't think Ken is one of them.

Ken said that my life, what I told him of it, is impressive. When I mentioned my master's thesis, the effect of fin-de-siècle American politics, fashion, and religious trends on James Joyce's *Ulysses*, he said he knew I'd end up in something like that. I think he meant *esoteric*, but he didn't use the word. He beamed that his hunch had been right. He asked about Steve, quite late in the conversation, and I told him Steve was a wonderful husband. It was probably the wrong thing for me to say, for it set up a hurdle that Ken, or any man, might feel is insurmountable.

Ken asked if I date much. I said I don't have a big field of men to choose from because most single men, by our age, have already been married and divorced. He understands about the Church's laws on marriage and divorce, having been brought up Catholic himself, and in fact he's still a churchgoer.

Sakiko had run to the supermarket after dropping me off and was already parked outside waiting for me when Ken told me he makes good money, has many safe investments, and would consider moving back to the States if he thought there was any hope for the two of us. He said he has never gotten over me and that I was the only girl he ever fell in love with. He said he regrets not keeping up our correspondence, but with his family's moving around so much he figured he was doing me a favor by exiting my life. I was stunned, not only by his carrying a torch, but by his candor. He asked if he could see me again.

There was a moment tonight, as I looked across at Ken and remembered the boy I dated in high school, remembered his kisses, his caresses, that tenderness beneath his virile exterior, well, there was a moment when I thought we might still have something together. There was an instant when I imagined myself married to Ken, the two of us making a home in Osaka or Nether Gorge, or somewhere else. There was a moment when I fantasized Ken's making love to me, in a grown-up and unhurried way, and I have to admit it was an exciting prospect, for I imagine Ken is still a man who wants to please his lover. In an instant all these thoughts went through my head, and I took Ken's hand in mine, in full view of his staff, his customers, his Japanese public. He didn't flinch.

So why did I tell Ken that all my time between now and when I leave next Monday is spoken for? He nodded, knowing I was lying, and I felt like a dog. He deserved better, he deserved the truth, but how could I tell him? How could I tell him why I wouldn't encourage him, why I couldn't see myself with him, why we would be wasting our time, how I would come to deride him, how our relationship would end in pain? How, how could I tell him, when it's hard for me to articulate it even to myself? Why would I hurt this man with the truth—this man whom I can still say I love?

And what is the truth? The truth is that Ken is just the same as he was twenty-five years ago. And that's the problem. Ken hasn't moved, he hasn't grown. I think that's just his personality, I think he's a man of things and not a man of thoughts. He talked about his business, about his vacations, about his apartment and the things he has in it. He never once spoke of ideas, of what isn't attached to this earth—of philosophy, literature, theology, art. I gave him several opportunities to discuss what matters to *me*, but, with the exception of acknowledging that we share a faith, he seemed at a loss to respond.

If that weren't enough, worse still is his complacency. Yes, he said he'd move for me, but if it weren't for me, what would he be doing for the rest of his life? What ambition does he have? How does he put himself at risk day to day? He kept emphasizing how stable he is, how he built up his shop slowly but surely, virtually positive every move was a smart one, leaving few things to chance, and he told me how he pretty much takes the same actions every day, and how that suits him. It's as though his skull has circumscribed his brain in cement, keeping old thoughts in and new thoughts out. Looking back, I knew when we were young that he had little interior life, but I was too naive, too unsophisticated, too passionate, to analyze the situation. It wasn't relevant to my life at the time, for Ken was otherwise attractive and fun. I don't think he'd be much fun for me now. He would bore me. He's stuck, and he's not about to change.

I could be making the biggest mistake of my life. I could be throwing away my last chance at happiness. Ken, knowing I was lying about being too busy to see him again, managed to say, a smile on his face, "You're still a terrible liar, Ginger." Ken laid himself bare to me, and I rejected him. I've burned my bridge.

When Sakiko picked me up she must have known things had gone poorly. I didn't say a word on the way back. She chatted on about how hard Mai studies and how hard Hiro works and how her job is to help them succeed. I wanted to yell at her, I wanted to say, "What about you? When will you do something for yourself?" but I held my tongue.

Back here in my room, before beginning this diary entry, I wrote out a few drafts of some verses. The poem is no great shakes, but I'll copy it here anyway. I won't let my critical brain get in the way of my expressive brain, for the verses capture how I feel tonight.

YIN/YANG

We are the two that cannot be one
I am the moon and you are the sun
I am the earth and you are the sky
You say *come near* and I say *good-bye*

We are the two that cannot be true
Orange is your color, and I prefer blue
You are the husband, I am the wife
You play for now, I play for life

Ours are two hearts that cannot be twined
Your body's your temple, my temple's my mind
I am your Venus, you are my Mars
We have our own lives, and those lives have scars

We are the two that cannot be one
You are the priest and I am the nun
You are the light and I am the shade
I am the forest, you are the glade

TWELVE
Chokoreto Keki

Celebrated on July 20 in the year 2000, Marine Day, also known as Ocean Day, is Japan's newest national holiday. It affords the private school students a break from rising early, sitting through lecture after lecture, and managing their homework. The students will meet their friends for picnics and restaurant meals. Municipal authorities will shoot off fireworks after sundown.

At home in suburban Osaka, Sakiko Murakami is busy in her modern kitchen, peeling potatoes, measuring flour, sugar, cocoa powder, and leavening, squinting at fine-print recipes her houseguest printed from the Internet. Ginger, in point of fact, is still in bed, recovering from her visit to the coffee shop. Sakiko shopped for groceries last night while Ginger conversed with Ken; she also bought a surprise for Ginger.

Once Sakiko has accomplished her preparation for the studio meal, she raps at Ginger's door and offers her guest a cup of coffee. Ginger has actually been awake for an hour, reading the book of poetry she found in her shoe cupboard yesterday at school. It's a volume of Edna St. Vincent Millay, in English, and inside the front cover are characters that Ginger cannot read, along with a finely written name in *romaji*: Sato Kaoru. Ginger has read "Interim" twelve times in this hour, struck by how Millay tells Ginger's story, although not precisely Ginger's story. Something is different.

Sakiko invites Ginger to come down for breakfast and the day's festivities. Nothing like appearing on television has happened to Sakiko before, and she has laundered and ironed her best cotton apron to wear over a new skirt and blouse. Her makeup and hair are *kanpeki*, as Ginger would say, and does.

"Today is big day, Ginger!"

"Hai."

"I have something to show you. Come down soon, please."

Ginger takes the stairs carefully and follows Sakiko into the kitchen.

"Here, Ginger, I have hair product for you."

"Like what?"

"Color. We are going to color hair."

"Mine?"

"What I use sometime. Pretty color. Little darker. Okay?"

Ginger can at least do this for Sakiko.

"What do I do?"

A short time later, compliments of Sakiko's dexterity with the creams and brush included in the box of Paon Seven-Eight Hair Color Cream in Natural Brown, applied for ten minutes, Ginger's hair is permanently several shades darker than her golden brown locks were, naturally. Sakiko blows Ginger's hair dry, using her fingers to separate the strands. Ginger's hair responds to Sakiko's styling by sticking out in wisps that threaten to topple over. Sakiko fine tunes her creation with her husband's hair gel. Sakiko has also purchased an eyeliner for Ginger in midnight black, and now she attends to her guest with it. "If you have dark contacts, you would be Japanese," Sakiko announces to Ginger at the end of her ministrations. Ginger looks from the neck up like a punk rocker.

The cooking show will be taped this afternoon, then edited and aired this evening. The segment is only a half hour long, which is barely time for Ginger to explain the ingredients in the dishes that she and Sakiko are presenting, much less time for the dishes to cook. Two hours have been allotted to a kitchen stage and a full crew, and after a manic Hiro rushes the women to the studio, Ginger and Sakiko are dusted with powder and let loose in front of the lights to start cooking.

The first order of business is to get the chicken on the grill, a domed contraption a stagehand has rigged up to mimic a Weber.

"You like my vent?" he asks the women, pointing to a tin apparatus snaking up from the grill and through a hole in the ceiling's acoustical tiles.

The cameras roll.

"At an American barbecue," Ginger announces, momentarily unconcerned about safety, "the first thing you do is drink a half a can of beer," and her cooking show begins with her quaffing several ounces from a tumbler bearing the studio's name. Ginger sets her half-empty beer can on the rack above the hot charcoals, and Sakiko, grimacing, whether from the physical struggle or from a distastefulness she may feel, pushes the chicken down onto the can. Sitting upright, headless, the bird looks like a soldier in an army, having made his supreme sacrifice for his country but still standing, as a good fellow would be if he could be. Ginger pours another beer, this time an entire can, into her glass. "You must drink beer while the chicken is cooking." Ginger smiles broadly. "It's part of the recipe," she adds.

Sakiko covers the grill with the domed lid and brings forth the potatoes she boiled and onions she chopped at home. She sets about mixing up the dressing for the potato salad, while Ginger, who could find no information online about the origins of potato salad, talks about the origin of the potato itself. This she combines with a short speech on the cultivation of corn and its value in the American diet—for corn oil, corn syrup, corn chips, and popcorn. She opens her third can of beer. Sakiko has put the cornbread in to bake and is now mixing up the chocolate cake, which Ginger grandly refers to in katakana English as *chokoreto keki*. For her part, Ginger is washing lettuce leaves and lining up bottles of olive oil, vinegar, and seasonings. All the while, camera operators film the women from angles both direct and oblique.

As the food cooks, Ginger's barbecue banter continues. The producer has joined the women on the stage and is interviewing them.

"Surely you've been on television before, Mrs. Oniru?" The producer's accent is thick. Ginger struggles to understand him.

"Only on Romper Room."

"Rompa Rumu?"

"A kid's show. I was on it in Cleveland with my sister, way back when."

"Child star. So today you are fixing American barbecue for us?"

"Hai, but I could only do it with my friend Sakiko's help."

"Hai, I help Ginger-san. She is good houseguest. We have fun time together."

"And you are in Japan to visit the school where the husband of Mrs. Murakami teaches?" the producer asks Ginger.

"That's right. I'm ambassador from school in Virginia."

"I'm sure you are a successful ambassador. Did anyone give you advice today, before the show?"

Ginger lets out a hiccup. "Sumimasen."

"Would you like another beer?" The producer motions the camera operators to move in closer.

"Yes, thanks you," Ginger slurs. "I never has enough to drink. I was little nervoush. When Hiro, my host man, drove us to station, he said I be myself on TV. 'Act natural, Jinja,' he said. *Konnichiwawa*, Hiro-san."

With her friend's speech complete, Sakiko jumps up to check on the chicken, the corn bread, and the baking cake, and pulls a brown-around-the-edges pan of corn bread from the oven. "Keki is ready soon, Ginger-san," she announces. "Chicken in some minutes, too."

Ginger stretches her arms over her head and asks if the cameras are still rolling.

"They are," says the producer, and introduces the guests joining them for the meal. Ginger is happy to see Junko, and they bow to each other. Accompanying Junko is a big man who is vaguely familiar to Ginger. He shakes hands with her.

"How nice to see you again, Mrs. O'Neill."

"Where do I know you from?"

"I believe the flight to Tokyo, Madam. You were on my lap."

Ginger dresses the salad with extra shakes of balsamic vinegar, an ingredient for which Sakiko paid an exorbitant price last night. Sakiko has kept a careful accounting of her expenses for the show, excluding Ginger's hair coloring and eyeliner, and slides an unmarked envelope containing her receipts across the table to Junko. The three women and two men have taken their seats in the air-conditioned, slightly smoky sound stage of the Kansai television station, prepared to enjoy a typical American backyard barbecue. Only the American is wise to the fact that the meal is bound to be a disaster.

Thursday, July 20 (Marine Day)

I look like a freak. Safety pins in my ears would complete the Gothic victim ensemble. I want Sakiko to think I like this pasty face topped with a clump of French-roasted coffee bean hair—I wouldn't hurt her for the world—but I did ask Hiro and her if we could stop at the drug store on the way home from the fireworks. I bought a bottle of darker foundation. I also picked up another pair of sunglasses.

We watched the cooking show before going out to see the *hanabi* shot off. I almost couldn't look at the TV, but Sakiko was taping it so I knew I'd have to see it eventually. I had such a headache from the beer, and my feet were swollen, so Sakiko plied me with pain-killers and tea and insisted I sit with my feet up, on Hiro's ottoman. She put Mai's socks on me, and we were like a family, the four of us sitting there in front of the TV. I felt safe and happy, especially as the half-hour episode progressed and I found that my idiocy had been edited from the show.

The nicest thing about the show was that my voice was never heard—except for my messed-up Japanese greeting to Hiro—I'd managed to add an extra syllable to my *Konnichiwa*. (Naturally that was the only line the editors kept in my voice.) Even Sakiko's comments were handled with voice-overs by Japanese professionals. I liked Sakiko's stand-in voice much better than mine; mine was much too low to be believable as coming from my body. My little burp, my large hiccup, and those garbled, incoherent words I emitted during filming went missing somewhere in audio editing, thank goodness. Except for the crazy way I looked, as if I'd had a bad shock on the way into the studio, we were brilliant. They cut out the camera close-ups of the burnt cornbread and the undercooked chicken and of Junko's pouring water on the chicken fat fire that was smoking up the studio. (That bogus Weber was malfunctioning; the chicken looked done to me.) Instead, they showed us merrily picking at the poultry skin with our fingers and downing whiskey sours, which Herr Berg had whipped up on the adjoining sound stage. I couldn't believe he was there, of all people—the story is he likes the station's programming and is studying it for the station he manages in his home port of Hamburg, which, incidentally, he invited me to visit at my earliest opportunity. I could be paranoid and argue that he's following me. He told me he'd show me around Germany. I'm sure—Germany and where else? Sakiko, too, could come, he said. Sakiko couldn't stop laughing at the prospect of *that*, but of course that part of our conversation was cut from the broadcast version.

The principal phoned as soon as the show was over and asked to speak to me. He said his family enjoyed the show and that he was looking forward to seeing me tomorrow at a meeting of the exchange committee. He said it would be the last one I'd be attending. He also said it's nothing I should worry about but that a school from

Texas has been in touch with him about a partnership—they'd caught wind of Confederate's bid and wanted to outplay (my word) us. How typically Texan! I told the principal I am sure Confederate is the best partner school his committee could find anywhere and that tomorrow I'd be at the committee's disposal to answer any remaining questions.

I lied when I told the principal that Confederate is the best partner his school could want. What makes Confederate better than any other school? We're not particularly nice people at Confederate—we'll stab you when you're not looking. And with Walk's public humiliation and marital disaster, he might not be long for the region. Who knows if a successor principal would even support the program? Then there's our technology faculty; they operate in the Dark Ages, although I've professed here that Confederate's computer system is state-of-the-art. We also have an aging—in other words, *old*—faculty, many of whom will be retiring in the next few years, and that leaves plenty of room for fresh, young personnel. Fresh and young, yes, but inexperienced. All this and more damning evidence I thought about as I sang our praises to the principal, so what was coming out of my mouth bore no relation to what was going through my head. Maybe everything I say is a lie. But I want to win this school. I need it for my self-respect, if nothing else.

I'm putting this journal down. I'm tired of it.

Friday, July 21

My last day of school! (Teachers are just as happy as students to see school end.) I'm not expected to show up tomorrow for the half day, and my plane leaves Monday morning.

For a change I was invited to the staff party after school. It would have been hard for them to exclude me from this one, given that it was specifically for me. We paraded down to the local bar, where the keg was freshly tapped and the noodles cooked, all of the expenses headed for the principal's tab. I took a lot of good-natured ribbing about the show yesterday; whether from Hiro's role as town crier or because it was obvious, my colleagues commented on the less-than-sober condition I was in and how the food could not have been edible. Even the chocolate cake, which I was sure would turn out perfectly, was soggy in the middle, the cake collapsing on our plates as Sakiko served it. I had spent some minutes on the show, most of which was cut, talking about the popularity of lava cake in the States. That's probably what a lava cake is anyway, an underdone chocolate cake.

The TV show wasn't all I was kidded for at the party. The other is much more serious. It could be damning. At the meeting today, the exchange committee asked more questions about Confederate, and then, late in the action, the social studies chairman said, "Given the class observations you've made over the time you've been here,

Mrs. O'Neill, what would you say about our style of teaching, as it compares to the American style? We want your honest opinion."

I complimented him on asking a very pertinent question, one that is important to ask given the close relationship that all of our students will have with teachers from the other school. I said it was clear the teachers here had a superb command of their subject matter, and that I knew the Confederate students would be in good hands if they were to attend classes here. The committee sat nodding their heads, looking in general pleased with themselves, although I did notice Akira looking somewhat circumspect, as though he was waiting for me to drop the other shoe. I had tried not to look at him at all, but I couldn't help a quick glance as I spoke. I wanted to meet the eyes of each of the committee members.

At that point, I had a choice to make. I know the Japanese don't come right out and say bad things; they dance around the point instead. I remembered why I'd been chosen for the ambassadorship. Saying the right thing has always been easy for me to do—little lies slip off my tongue the way fatty tuna slides down my throat. But I saw myself standing there, from the point of view of the others at the meeting, and I knew what they deserved from me. The committee members deserved the truth from me, not some easy-to-digest pabulum that would make everyone feel good but that didn't reflect reality. I decided to say what I thought, even though it would be hard, even if it cost me what I came to Japan for.

So I spoke the truth, at last. I said the Japanese practice of straight and relentless lecture, without group discussion, without projects for the students to work on, and without any variety in instructional tools and methods, well, it was not the best of pedagogical models. There was dead quiet in the room as I spoke, except for Teru's trying to interrupt me, but the principal told him to let me continue. I went on to say that I thought our Confederate students would benefit from the partnership, even though they would find the educational method stultifying, but that I had concern about the Japanese students who would be coming to Confederate. My concern was that they would experience a more open educational environment in the United States and so would forever be dissatisfied with the droning by which they are expected to learn here at home. I said I had been asked for my honest opinion, and that's what I was giving them.

Oddly, I didn't feel the urge to take my remarks back. I'm a fast thinker; I could have changed my mind. I could have claimed that based on their stunned silence, I was sure the committee had misunderstood me, that I would explain it another way, and then I could have changed my tune slightly, convincingly. I know how to do that, but I didn't want to. I wanted to stand by the truth.

No one said a word—not I, not the social studies head, not even the principal. And after all I've been through on this trip—bleeding on the principal's furniture, the aborted tryst with Akira, the scare I had with Bernie, fending off Walk and the *Post* reporter every day—you'd think I would deserve to go home with a victory. But in reality, I deserve nothing, not the way a child deserves food for her belly, or a mother deserves good prenatal care, or a father deserves not to lose a son in battle. I don't deserve a damned thing. I had hoped I would go home with my head held high, giving me a moment of achievement, something I could be proud of. But, as I've said, pride is a sin, and besides, grace is given, not earned. Not deserved.

Saturday, July 22

Sakiko and I spent the day shopping. She bought a *wanpisu*—a one-piece dress. She also bought a *shatsu*—a shirt—for Hiro. And I've been complaining about the direction of the *English* language! The Japanese are leaving us in the dust with their spurious vocabulary additions. I did give Sakiko a laugh today when I called lunch *hiro-gohan*. She corrected me—it's *hiru-gohan*. Nothing like a little cannibalism, eating my host.

I bought some little ceramic dishes, for appetizers and snacks and the like. They don't come in sets of four but in sets of five. Four is an unlucky number. Its homophone means *death*. One of the sets is for Reggie and one for me. I picked up a pair of earrings for Bernie—dangly silver gingko leaves. The clerks in the shops thanked us over and over for our business, a change from Nether Gorge where more often than not customers find themselves thanking clerks for letting them buy something instead of the other way around.

This morning I had what I hope is my last e-mail from Sir Walk. He said there will be a school contingent to meet my plane, along with press and a representative from the Japanese embassy. If it wouldn't mess up Hiro and Sakiko's plans to run me to Kansai Airport Monday morning, I'd change to an earlier flight and cab it home from the airport.

Over lunch Sakiko pointed out that I seemed to have gotten over Akira easily. She wondered aloud if I truly had put him in my past. She knew Ken hadn't worked out, so she was surprised I wasn't brooding about Akira. I asked her what there was to brood about—our relationship was ill-fated, ill-meant, ill-played-out. There was nothing good about it. She didn't look as though she was buying the story; she raised her eyebrows and said, "Are you sure, Ginger?" I assured her I was sincere, but she harped on about how sometimes our wishes are unconscious and that maybe a part of me was in mourning for what could have been a fulfilling relationship. "You are person who needs intimacy, Ginger," she said. "But you wear mask." I didn't like being psychoanalyzed and told her she was wrong. I'm content as I am.

In fact, since the trip to Awaji, I haven't spoken to Akira and have avoided not only the music room but also that entire wing. Yesterday I found a note in my slipper cupboard when I arrived at school. It read:

To Ginger:

I understand things worked out for you and your daughter. I'm sorry you were upset with me. I have been busy with family matters and will be in touch.

Akira

I didn't tell Sakiko about this. It didn't mean anything, wasn't worth mentioning. But then after dinner tonight the phone rang. Hiro took the call.

"Jinja, I have a message for you. From *Sensei*." Hiro was standing in the doorway, looking at his wife, not at me. I'd had my head buried in Millay. I knew exactly who he meant by *Sensei*.

"Yes?"

"*Sensei* has been given opera tickets for the Sunday matinee and wants you to go with him. He asks also if you are available for lunch beforehand."

"My husband has become go-between," Sakiko said, punching at her calculator as she worked at her checkbook.

"Sakiko, you and I talked about driving out to the countryside on my last day here."

"It's your decision. Trip to country would be for you, not for me. Which do you prefer?"

What I wanted was not to make a fool of myself again. "If it's just lunch and the opera, I suppose that's okay," I told Hiro, knowing I could give no other answer. Akira and I have issues to settle between us. "How can it be any worse than what's happened already?" I meant the question rhetorically, but Sakiko took it up.

"You would not want anything worse to happen."

"Did he say which opera is playing?" I asked Hiro.

"He didn't. Do you want me to find out?"

"It doesn't matter," I said. "Tell him I'll go."

"That's what I told him you would say," Hiro replied and left the room.

"I don't plan to let this thing get out of hand again, Sakiko," I said. "We'll just have a teachers' outing. A cultural excursion."

"You don't need to explain to me."

"I've made a resolve, and it's better for me if I articulate it, give it some substance by putting it into words." I shut my book and dried my palms on my slacks. "You must think I'm a terrible person."

"No. I think you are having romance," Sakiko said. "First romance in very long time."

"But I could have picked a more, how should I say, available man. It's not fair to Akira's wife."

"People do not look for particular type of person to love."

"But I could refuse his overtures instead of accepting them."

"Couple could have agreement. Understanding."

"Meaning?"

Sakiko shut her checkbook. "I will tell you something, Ginger. When I called Megumi-san that night to find you and Akira-san, she was not surprised you are with her husband. As a matter of fact, Megumi-san was very gracious."

"She was saving face. Isn't that a common Japanese thing to do?"

"Maybe she is glad to have someone for her husband to spend his energy with."

"How could Megumi not want him?"

"She may want him, but sometime Japanese woman doesn't want to do sex with husband."

"If she wants him at all, isn't she entitled to all of him?"

"You can give Akira-san something his wife does not want to give him."

I did not want to insult her and her culture by saying I don't intend to be Akira's concubine. Eastern marriages are beyond my experience. I restated my original notion. "I don't plan to end up in bed with him."

Sakiko shook her head, and I sensed her impatience. We had said all there was to say. She rose, bade me sweet dreams, and went up to her room.

THIRTEEN

Fugu

"You've never had *fugu*?"

"Isn't that the fish that kills you before you've stood up from the table?"

"Only if the chef doesn't know what he's doing."

Ginger should be thinking about what she's doing, but she's not being particularly sensible right now, not about the big issues, that is.

"What's the big deal with fugu? Why would you put your life on the line for a piece of fish? It's not on the menu at the restaurants I eat at back home, but I've heard of a place nearby that serves it. There's an English word for it, isn't there?"

"Blowfish. It's especially delicious, that's why people take the risk. It's very light, like an angel's kiss."

Ginger conjures up an image of Akira holding a slice of blowfish between his chopsticks, pregnant for her mouth.

"Why don't you order it, then, if it's that good? Is it on the menu here?"

Akira laughs. "Yes, but it's too expensive. I only eat it when my rich uncle takes me out."

Ginger nods and attends to her *unaju*. Her meal is an orgy of sushi served in a bowl, grilled eel on a bed of rice, sweetened sauce brushed over the fish. She ordered the one-layer bowl. It's unlikely she'll be able to eat all of it. Akira had asked her if there was anything else she wanted to eat before she leaves Japan. Ginger mentioned *aji*. Akira told her this restaurant doesn't specialize in horse mackerel, and he wouldn't recommend ordering it.

"But when you visit next time, we'll go out for it." Akira uses his fingers to pick up a deep-fried tofu pocket filled with sushi rice. "Sushi can be habit forming, Ginger. By the way, did you know *inari-zushi* is named after Inari, the god of grain? Remember the fox shrine in Kyoto? Foxes are messengers of Inari. They guard Inari shrines."

"Everything's got to do with food, hasn't it?" Ginger says, all but shoveling unaju into her mouth. "But speaking of sightseeing, Sakiko took me to Osaka Castle yesterday after lunch. Its inside is markedly different from its outside."

"Oh?" Akira looks interested.

"The outside walls are brilliant and patinated, and of course it was hot outside yesterday, late in the afternoon, but inside we were in comfort. It was nice and cool."

"That's the value of no-tech air conditioning."

"Right. We spent some time looking at the displays and then wandered into what Sakiko said is the famous golden tearoom. Everything in it is golden," Ginger says, forgetting that Akira must know all this, "the walls, the ceiling, all the tools for the tea ceremony."

"It isn't authentic, Ginger. The inside was gutted and the museum built fresh."

"Oh. Like Disney World."

"Sort of. What are you reading now?"

"Edna St. Vincent Millay. By the name on the endpaper, I figured it was you who put the book in my cupboard. Who is Kaoru?"

"My mother."

"I'll have Hiro get the book back to you."

"I want you to have it, Ginger. My mother's dead, and you're the first person I've met who will enjoy it as much as she did."

"Thank you."

"New hair? You look Japanese."

Akira asks for the menu again. In Japanese style, he orders courses seriatim so as to have his meal as fresh as possible. He places an order for two pieces of battleship-style nigiri sushi, topped with ikura. "For our memories, Ginger," he says. "And when you return to Japan, we can visit castles together. It's always enjoyable to see them through the eyes of a friend."

"What makes you think I'll come back?" Strangely, Ginger's question sounds both coy and argumentative.

"Haven't you enjoyed your visit?"

"Of course I have. It's just that I don't know what the future holds." What she really wonders is what it holds for them. "Would you like me to come back?"

"Obviously."

"Why obviously?"

"Can't you tell I've enjoyed your visit?"

"Actually I was flabbergasted you wanted to see me again. After I made such a scene at the ferry."

"I'm sorry, Ginger," Akira says. "You were under a lot of stress, and I should have been more considerate. I'm afraid I'm not used to thinking of others."

"We were caught in an unfortunate situation." Gingers sips her Chardonnay and returns the glass to the table, stroking the stem. "Did you enjoy the Watanabe exhibit?"

"The gallery was closed. The owner had gone to Hokkaido on holiday."

"Another time, then," Ginger says.

"That's something you can look forward to doing with me when you come back."

"What else can I look forward to with you?"

"What do you mean?"

Even someone who is acting as recklessly as Ginger is needs to know how Akira has sized her up, what he expects of her. "I'm not interested in being someone's mistress, you know," she tells him.

"Did I ever say anything about your being my mistress?"

"It's the implication, isn't it? I mean, what intentions do you have for our relationship?"

"I thought we'd let things happen as they are meant to."

"What does that mean?"

"Nothing in particular. Whatever makes you happy, Ginger. I don't put any burdens on you, do I?"

Akira sounds so casual, but maybe that's how things are in his world, with his kind of relationships. When the waitress comes with the bill, Ginger sets a large-denomination note on the table and pushes it toward Akira, having no idea how the note compares to the amount of the bill. Akira pushes the money back at her.

"Ginger, that's not necessary. Let this be my treat."

"No," she insists, pushing the money back at him. "You'll take it, because I never had the chance to pay for my share at the ryokan. Or for the ferry."

"The trip was my gift to you." He lays his hand on hers. "But okay, I understand you. Thank you for lunch."

Now that Akira has agreed with her, she withdraws her hand from under his, but she does it reluctantly. She wants Akira to touch her. How is it that with her hand on Ken's Wednesday night, Ginger felt in her body only the sensations she picked up on her skin itself, that is, the warmth and roughness of Ken's own hand, but when Akira's hand touches hers, she senses movement in parts of her body far away from her skin, parts deep inside her?

Ginger, what good can come of this day?

"Akira, tell me about the opera we'll see this afternoon."

"You could call *Prince Igor* a bit of a problem." The couple is on foot, on their way to Festival Hall. "There's little agreement among musicologists on the order of the scenes."

"The composer didn't number the scenes?"

"Borodin didn't finish the opera. Rimsky-Korsakov and Glazunov put it in order, orchestrated it, and wrote the overture. Each director must resolve the ambiguities all over again."

"This is my first *Igor*, although I'm certainly familiar with the Polovtsian dances. Is there a literary source for the opera?"

"When you get home," Akira calls out as they cross traffic-jammed streets, "look for Nabokov's translation of *The Song of Igor's Campaign*. Keep in mind, though, that very little of the opera is based on the literary source."

"I'd like to get to Russia. Maybe next summer," Ginger says, although she's having trouble seeing that far ahead.

"See St. Petersburg, Ginger. It's a city of great beauty, although little charm. Anyway, it will be interesting to learn what order this director puts the scenes in." Akira takes Ginger's arm as they step up a curb. "Be sure, Ginger, that you listen for the *nyega*."

"The what?"

"Nyega." They are reaching the doors of the theater. "It means *bliss* to the Russians. You'll hear it, for example, in the undulations between the fifth and sixth degrees of the scale."

"I'll try, but I'm afraid you give me credit for more musical sophistication than I deserve."

"Just listen for the most sensuous, passionate music you can imagine."

The opera house is larger than any Ginger has ever been in. Their seats are in the first row—the couple is nearly on stage themselves. As the orchestra warms up, Akira translates from the Japanese program the synopsis and the order of scenes for Ginger. His mood changes steadily as he reads, from anticipation to confusion to exasperation. His teeth are clenched; he's breathing shallowly through them. Akira mutters in Japanese into his program booklet.

"What's wrong?"

"This is an insult."

"What do you mean?"

"This isn't how *Igor* should be performed. The order of scenes is criminal!"

Ginger looks at her appointment book to have something to do.

After several minutes of silence, Ginger says, "I meant to ask you, Akira, is this production Russian or Japanese? Or from some other country?"

"It's a Russian production, with a Russian company singing it." His mouth is set at an odd diagonal.

"Will it be sung in Russian, or in Japanese?"

"In Russian, unless I'm mistaken."

The house lights dim, and a middle-aged conductor appears at the podium. With pallid skin and wispy brown hair and dressed in a dark business suit, he is unremarkable until he raises his hands. Then, his arms making strokes that are full and certain, he puts the musicians under his power. The overture generates such a mix of major and minor passages that it twists both Ginger's mind and her senses around with the music. Whether she's facing a tragedy, a comedy, or something in between is beyond Ginger's guessing.

The main curtain rises onto a blank, moderately raked stage, the floor tipped down toward the audience. Riderless horses, projected as crisp shadows from behind a translucent screen, dance from right to left across the back of the stage, a blare of brass directing the listener to the racing stringed instruments. Downstage a rumpled bed rolls onto the stage, a man and woman on it, and, under blue light, the pulsing of the couple's lovemaking coincides with the phrasing of the orchestra and the rhythm of the horses. Akira draws his breath in sharply.

The Russian townsmen suit up for battle, and when the music turns threatening, the enemy—the Polovtsians— appear. They are bathed in the harshest and hottest of lights, a fluorescent orange. From their risers they are peering menacingly at the Russians. Lighting suggests the sun's eclipse, at first with the brightness of the intense orange, then with a darkening of cool blue, and yet again heating up with orange.

The Russian chorus sings a rousing *Slava* while the lovers, Prince Igor and his wife, Yaroslavna, orgiastically act out the singers' enthusiasm. The curtain drops for a scene change, and Ginger keeps her eyes on the conductor as he waits for his cue to resume the music. Ginger is afraid to look at Akira; she is both flustered and stimulated by the blatant sexuality of the opera. She is also reliving the confusion of feelings she had on Awaji Island when she and Akira were intimate. She dreads that her outward demeanor will betray how she feels inside, feelings she is working hard to censor.

With the curtain rising onto a new scene, the lighting is once more sun-colored, and the prince is lying on a divan in enemy camp, he and his son Vladimir having been captured during a military campaign. The bass Konchak, leader of the enemy Polovtsians, looks African, but the rest of the Polovtsians are made up in black-face. They look like something from the 1930s, ridiculous and in poor taste.

Konchak directs the slave women to entertain his captive guest, and the Polovtsian men join their women. The singers move around and between each other, the men's voices pressing on with priapic urgency, the women's voices weaving musical gauze to flatter the men's advances. Ginger hears themes from American musical theater, including *Kismet*'s "Stranger in Paradise," and she projects that she's a stranger in paradise herself. Nyega has been driven into every atom of this opera.

As the curtain falls for another scene change, Ginger tingles from the hard-driving percussion. The audience is loud, volatile, with talk. Akira turns to Ginger and nearly shouts, "Have you noticed there's no scenery?"

Ginger nods, but in fact she hadn't given the scenery any thought one way or another.

"This is Euro-trash, Ginger."

"What?"

"It's garbage. Do you want to leave?"

"No. I like it."

Akira crosses his arms, and Ginger crosses her legs. She is determined to see this to the end.

At the first intermission, Akira buys plastic cups of apple juice. Opera patrons in the lobby are chatting excitedly. Everyone except Akira seems in high spirits.

"The director should go back to school," Akira says.

"But don't you think the audience likes the production? Except for the tacky lighting, I'm enjoying it," Ginger says.

"This production is blatantly carnal. It patronizes the Japanese people. The music Borodin wrote is lovely enough. There don't need to be all these distractions to take away from the music and drama."

"You said yourself Borodin didn't finish organizing the opera, so what upsets you about the scene order?"

"It's not just the scene order, Ginger. There's a lot more than that going on."

"You've said. How do you think it should be directed?"

Akira doesn't have a chance to answer, for just then he and Ginger are approached by another couple. It's the principal and his wife. The principal's wife compliments Ginger on the cooking show. The principal excuses himself to buy drinks. His wife says something to Akira in Japanese, which brings a look over Akira's face Ginger hasn't seen on him before. She can't make out whether he's bewildered or embarrassed. He doesn't reply, and the woman walks away to join her husband in line.

"What was that all about?"

"Nothing," Akira says, looking away. "But you asked what I would be doing differently in this production, Ginger. To start with, the lighting is canned, the costumes look as though they have been lying in a musky basement for most of the twentieth century, and the direction has been handled not musically but erotically." He speaks fast but softly, and by the end is again looking into Ginger's eyes.

Ginger refrains from telling Akira that the word he's looking for is *musty* and that he's only said how the production shouldn't be done, not how he might direct it.

"Not only that, Ginger, but the cast is broken down by race. I would have thought the opera world was beyond that."

"Isn't this a period opera?"

"Then the Russians should be European and the Polovtsians Asian, not African. The production shouldn't be playing into stereotypes, much less nonsensical ones."

Akira might have a point, yet Ginger still likes the show. "I think it's interesting to see how a director can put something like this together in a new and unusual way," she says. In her cup of juice, she sees the reflections of the lobby's lights, then swallows the golden fluid. "Art is supposed to do that, to make you think of things in a new way."

Akira rubs his ear and looks unconvinced.

"This director," Ginger continues, "he's exploring the boundaries of otherness, don't you think?"

"I don't know."

"I saw a production of *Othello*, the play, not the opera," Ginger goes on, "where Othello was the only light-skinned person in the cast; everyone else was dark-skinned. It was very effective."

"That's different. That's a story about race."

"I thought it was about a jealous husband." Ginger doesn't know herself where she's headed with her argument.

"A woman's view," Akira says.

"Maybe. Or maybe something else, something common to both genders. Infidelity." Finally, Ginger has made her point.

"I'll have to think about that."

"Well, it's obvious to me, but while you think, I'm going to the women's room. Maybe I'll find a group of your old girlfriends in there, talking about us. I'll see you at the seat." At this rate, the parting will be easier.

Akira isn't at his seat when Ginger returns to hers. The house lights dim, and as the spotlight finds the conductor, Akira enters from the far side of the house and crosses along the first row, in front of Maestro Yurinsky. Akira's face is momentarily in the conductor's spotlight as the audience warmly applauds. By the time Akira takes his seat, Ginger, having witnessed his entrance with dismay, is scrunched down in hers. Surely Akira has acted consciously to insult the opera company.

On stage, Igor appears in a russet light. He's far from home and deep in lamentation for having failed his people. His wretchedness is palpable to Ginger. This young baritone, the singer—not the character—must have done something in his own life that has led him to experience grief and humiliation; he appears to grasp it well in the character he's portraying. His voice reminds Ginger of Akira's. The fact of the matter is that everything makes Ginger think of Akira. Akira's body, which seemed so strange to her on Awaji, is familiar by now, his face, his arms, his neck, and his chest having been at every moment since that warm night somewhere in Ginger's consciousness.

The music pours itself into the audience, into Ginger, as the boyars enter to report to Yaroslavna that Igor has been captured and that the Polovtsians are marching on their city. Yaroslavna's grief and guilt parallel her husband's; she faints upon hearing the enemy is coming for her. The boyars follow with a procession of icons and crosses, heralding the message of God's wrath and punishment, and those articles look heavy and sharp, their jagged metal pressing on Ginger's chest. She associates the religious props with the Spanish Inquisition, and with a faith's bearing down. She also associates them with Steve's death, and the weight that crushed him.

At the second intermission Akira begs Ginger's pardon for his earlier pique, then complains that Konchakovna, Konchak's daughter and Vladimir's love interest, should already have made her vocal appearance. "I can't believe the Japanese people are paying for this."

"What do you mean? The audience loves it."

"I mean this production is underwritten by Japanese organizations and a Japanese company."

"But what do you think of the singers?"

Akira smiles for the first time since he looked at his program. "Igor looks too young for the role, and his voice is coming under some strain." His eyes on Ginger's lips, he adds, "But he has good phrasing. Good breath control."

"I wish the Polovtsians were singing in a language other than Russian. I wish there were a language gap between them and the Russians."

"That's an interesting idea, Ginger, but why would you want there to be a language gap?"

"It would highlight their differences and be more realistic. I'm always put off at performances of *Madama Butterfly*. Both American and Japanese characters, who presumably are communicating in each other's languages, sing in Italian. I like Italian, but it's foolish in that setting." Akira begins to speak, but Ginger cuts him off. "I wish the cast sang some of the arias in Japanese and some in English. I keep going to *Madama Butterfly*, hoping to hear it sung that way."

"*Butterfly* is overrated, but it's sung in the right language. The composer's wishes should be respected. Puccini was Italian."

"I know he was Italian. But you're missing my point." They are arguing again. "It's too bad you aren't enjoying the opera, Akira." *We aren't suited to each other*, Ginger says to herself.

"Oh, don't worry." Akira reaches out and touches her arm. "I can enjoy productions I object to as much as ones I approve of. They give me more to criticize. And of course I enjoy your company," he adds. One thing can be said for Akira. He's never boring.

It's evening in the enemy camp as the last act opens on a chorus of Polovtsian maidens. The lighting crew is busy—hackneyed lighting or not. The hot oranges and reds sway even more with the singing than do the maidens. The throbbing instrumental drone, a repetitive rhythm to which the women are moving their hips, puts Ginger under a spell. Akira has raised his hands to his temples.

Konchakovna, at last making her entrance, is rolled in from the wings upon a heavily draped platform bed, and like Konchak, she is of African descent. Her hair is long, in ringlets off her face, a face that is wide and soft. She wears barely anything, akin to Maria Ewing in the *Salomé* that Ewing's husband directed. Akira has dropped his hands into his lap.

Konchakovna's contralto bewitches Ginger, the motifs of her cavatina building on what's gone before. The singer is anticipating her lover, and by the end of her song Konchakovna is squirming on her satin sheets. The Russian prisoners, including Vladimir and his father, swarm onto the stage under Polovtsian guard, and Konchakovna shows her maidens how they are to comfort the Russian men. A bacchanal follows, gradually progressing upstage, but Vladimir withdraws from the group and moves downstage for his cavatina. It's clear he hungers for Konchakovna, who is tangled up with the chorus, but he looks away from the contralto, right at Ginger, and sings to her, long enough to make Ginger uncomfortable.

Konchakovna has freed herself from the ensemble and is again lying on her bed. Vladimir spies her and goes to her. Now the lighting is incandescent and subtle, the oboe heralding the young lovers' bliss. During their duet it's hard to make out whose limbs are whose and even whose voice is whose. Konchakovna sings up to Vladimir, then down again as his voice tops hers, and so on as they vocally tease each other until the lovers' voices have blended into one expression. They are finally singing *with* each other, not *at* each other, their bodies mirroring their voices.

The stage goes dark as the bed is rolled off, replaced with the Polovtsian army singing a victory song. Vladimir, Igor, and the rest of the Russian prisoners enter, aware that their city has been taken by enemy forces. Igor is ashamed of himself for his losses. Vladimir hasn't his father's patriotism; the boy's fresh romantic interests lie elsewhere than at home. Igor manages an escape, but Vladimir shows ambivalence when caught in a net that drops from the flies above. Ginger identifies with the young man's failure to protest his circumstances, with the contradiction of his wanting and not wanting something, and with his tempting fate, tasting forbidden fruit. Konchakovna throws herself in front of Vladimir to save him from the angry Polovtsians. Her father directs his men to spare Vladimir, then joins his daughter's and the young man's hands, blessing them with a salaam. At the curtain, the cool lighting for a last time suggests Russia, where Igor is returning to his wife, and where the chorus is once again singing *Slava*.

The house has erupted. Behind Ginger and Akira a host of patrons rises to its feet. Akira is ashen, and stays seated. When the conductor takes his curtain call, holding the hands of Yaroslavna and Vladimir, Ginger stands to applaud, shedding tears for the first time since she kissed Bernie good-bye at the airport three weeks ago.

Akira stands. "You okay, Ginger?"

"Fine. You?"

"I have a headache. A migraine." He says it *mee-graine*.

The applause goes on, but Akira has taken Ginger's hand and is leading her out of the hall. "I can find my way home, take a cab, maybe," she offers. Akira was to see her home the same way they came, by train. His car is parked at the station. It took them an hour to get from the station to the restaurant, with two train changes, and Ginger isn't anxious to try to negotiate the system on her own. "I'd call Sakiko," she says, "but they were all taking the day to visit Hiro's brother and his family. They gave me a key. They might be late."

They are now out in the hot, late sun, and still Ginger is talking. "They wouldn't have gone if I hadn't come with you. They would have spent my last day with me."

Akira has hailed a cab and is waiting for the driver to open the door. The couple climbs in, and Akira speaks to the driver.

"Ginger, under the circumstances, I hope you won't think badly of me if we find a place where I can rest. I'll see you home when I'm feeling better."

"Of course, whatever you think is best," she says, but where is this place where Akira will rest? "Is there anything I can do?"

"No. I have an injection that will cure it." He looks over at her. "Don't worry. I'm not a drug addict. It's just for migraines."

"Do you get a lot of them?"

"Enough that I know what to do. You'll forgive me if I sit quietly now. The lights and noise in the opera were driving me crazy." He pulls out his ironed handkerchief, unfolds it, leans his head back on the seat, and lays the cloth over the top of his face. "Color and music are both vibrations," he adds.

Ginger attempts to relax as the minutes and city scenery pass. This is an unfamiliar area of Osaka. In ten minutes the cab comes to a stop next to a squat, ugly building, marked already, before sunset, by flashing neon lights. Most of the surrounding structures are lit in the same way. Akira snaps to attention to pay the driver.

When he gets out of the cab, he slides smoothly across the seat, while Ginger's bare legs stick to it.

"Where are we?"

"Don't worry. We'll be here only a short time," Akira replies, and leads the way into the building. They are alone in a foyer, and ahead of them is a mirrored window behind a narrow counter. There's a gap below the window to slide money through, as at a bank or a gas station in the States. Ginger can't see who is on the other side.

"What is this place?"

Akira speaks into the microphone at the window and then looks at the wall next to him. Plastic squares form a grid on the wall, eight squares by eight. Some squares are lit from behind and some are dark. Each of the lighted squares shows a numbered room, with a photograph of that room. Each room is a bedroom.

"Akira, where are we?"

"We're here because I need to lie down, and I don't want our time together to end because of my headache." He passes cash under the mirror and gets a key in return. Ginger's nose is shiny in her reflection.

"Don't tell me this is one of those love hotels I've heard about." She's read that even married couples come to places like this, for privacy.

Akira doesn't reply.

The person in the booth buzzes the lock on the door to a hallway, and from there the couple takes the elevator to the third floor. That hallway is dark except for miniature lights around the frames of a few of the doorways. Akira stops at one of the doors and opens it. The doorway lights go out. Ginger's mind races. How did she end up here? Does she want to be here? If she didn't want to be here, she'd leave. No one is holding a gun to her head. Surely she can think of the right thing to do.

Faithful reader, the moment has come at which your narrator must take a bow. Ginger will continue this journey on her own. Ginger knows the rules; she grasps the received wisdom about relationships, about fair play, about the implications of making choices. She can weigh the good of the community against the good of the individual. She has a strong and well-formed conscience, a sense of right and wrong that has been taking shape inside her since she was a child. Now is the time for Ginger to go deep into herself, into and beyond her senses, into and beyond her intellect, and into her subconscious, into that place where Ginger never lets anyone go, hardly even herself. It's time for her to mine that hidden earth and work the future out for herself. Ginger will be on her own for a time, but she will remember that no matter what she does, no matter how things turn out, her life is built on a foundation, and that foundation is a form of grace. Even if the decisions she makes in the next little while aren't the best of decisions, she can make them right. For Ginger must remember, as must you, faithful reader, that nobody is beyond redemption. Nobody.

We'll meet again, Ginger. When you're ready.

Sunday, July 23

The walls and ceiling in that room were mirrored, and the air smelled of disinfectant. The bed, extra-large and heart-shaped, like something out of a Pocono Mountains honeymoon suite, dictated the space. The bedspread was a hideous fabric, a quilted and silky purple. Pink toss pillows, also heart-shaped, decorated the head of the bed. Akira moved the pink pillows onto a chair and pulled back the spread. Beneath it were pink satin sheets and plump bed pillows. He drew shut the blackout draperies and went into the bathroom, closing the door behind him.

I took the pillows from the chair and set them on the small bureau next to the television set. Still standing, I picked up one of the magazines from the nightstand and paged through it, flipping past fashions and advertisements. I could read only brand names. Everything else was in Japanese characters.

When Akira returned from the bathroom, he was wearing a white terrycloth bathrobe. He took off his watch, turned down the sheet, and got into bed. Soon he was snoring lightly. I wasn't sure what to do. Unlike the opera singers, Akira and I were there without a director. I went into the Western-style bathroom, the pink toilet no longer shocking. The maroon wall tiles made the small room seem even smaller than it was. Akira had hung his clothes on a hook on the back of the door. There was a second robe.

When I came out of the bathroom a half hour later, Akira's eyes were open. "You okay, Ginger?" he asked.

"Yes."

"I didn't expect to see you in the robe."

"I took a shower," I told him. "I'll get dressed in a few minutes. I thought I'd give my clothes a chance to lose some of their humidity. How are you feeling? You look better."

"I am much better. The medicine is a miracle drug." Akira smiled at me, making up for his crossness at the opera. "Thank you for understanding."

"You're welcome." I waited. He was silent. I fidgeted with the belt of my robe, trying to think, trying to work out my feelings for him, and then I found myself letting slip the one thing that was on my mind. "Did you have this planned?" I asked him. "Your headache, I mean? This hotel?"

"Are you joking?" he said, keeping his eyes on mine and moistening his lips with his tongue. "Do you think I brought you here to make love to you?"

I didn't know how to answer the question; somehow there was more than one level to it. Today I wanted to have more control over my impulses than I'd had on Awaji, but I'm sure I showed more control at the ryokan than Akira would have liked. How could I know what he really wanted, or expected? I stood mute.

"Don't make me out for Don Juan. You should know, Japanese men aren't hanging out with geishas all the time, regardless of the picture that's painted in Western culture."

"I know that. But what are we doing here?"

Akira took my hands and drew me to him.

"Ginger, Ginger, don't you see? I can't live without you."

For a moment I wasn't sure what Akira had said. I replayed it over and over, giving myself time to think, and in those moments I considered many things—my husband, my daughter, my faith, what my faith offers me, what my faith withholds from me.

"I can't go on without you," Akira repeated.

Knowing with every thread of my being that it was the wrong thing to do, I let Akira take me in his arms. Yet still I was desperate to exorcise hell's everlasting fire from my hyper-awareness, and so I prayed (*prayed!*) that God would deliver me from the earthquake that could come without warning, the earthquake brought on by my sinful behavior, the earthquake that would bury us alive. And then, with my lover's mouth meeting mine, my carnal self took over, and I managed to cast from my mind all thoughts but those of Akira, letting him move me far from my past, far from my future, far from my home. I had only the present, and I was present in it for him.

Akira shed his robe, and, in the fractured light from the edges of the window, I drank up his nakedness. I took the band from his ponytail and ran my hands through his thick, coarse hair. I massaged his scalp with my fingertips. "No one has ever touched me like this, Ginger," he said, and I was surprised.

Slowly Akira drew his fingers down the nape of my neck and around to my breasts. It has been so many years since I've been touched like that, and never exactly in the way he was touching me. His kisses found parts of my body I thought would never be kissed again. And then, after a while, he stopped.

"Don't stop," I said.

"Are you sure?"

My body was able to give Akira his answer. He opened the nightstand drawer and reached for a condom, hotel supplied. He looked at me with the intensity of the hot rays that lit the Polovtsian camp.

"I want to find my way into the white hot center of you," he said, and there was no turning back for either of us.

"There's been a space in me just waiting for you to fill," I told him, and he reached me at my core. I will never forget the chaos in my mind in those moments—visions of Yaroslavna and Igor and Konchakovna and Vladimir; memories of Ken and Steve; dreams of myself flying off into the future in the arms of a man I love.

In those first moments our kisses were long and languorous, and if I were to put it in musical terms, our lovemaking, that is, I would have to say we moved at a smoothly fashioned *andante amoroso*, then at an *allegro appassionata*, and, finally, in the joy of no longer holding each other back, we were *due corde*, two strings of a violin, sounding in unison.

We must have fallen asleep because when I next opened my eyes it was the neon lighting, not the sun, that was finding its way through the draperies.

"Ginger, we have so little time," were the words I awoke to. Akira's lips found mine, and neither my body nor my mind would refuse him. I wanted Akira to leave no void in me. I wanted him again and again. I yearned to be in a sea, in a sea of Akira and his life. I yearned for him to empty his saltiness over me, around me, into me. It was wrong to make love to this man, and I knew it, but unlike Friday at the committee meeting when I was determined to do the right thing, this evening I turned away from what I knew was right.

Akira buried his face in my neck. His hands were kneading me, and I was dissolving like a Dali timepiece. I was Akira's clay, he my potter. I was his nourishment, his sustenance, and he was mine.

"I love you," Akira said. He was humming Igor's theme. Already I was elsewhere, barely conscious, barely of this world. And, if I'd been counting, in what would have been six full beats—two measures of our waltz— Akira collapsed upon me.

(I hear the Murakamis coming in downstairs. I'll stay quiet here in my room. They'll see the slippers outside my door and assume I've gone to bed. I don't want to be interrupted. I have so much to write.)

"I don't want to leave you," I confessed to Akira, when I could again speak.

"You don't have to. Stay with me, Ginger."

"I have a daughter waiting for me. Anyway, what kind of life could I have here?"

"I'm afraid what I can offer you is inadequate. I wish I'd met you years ago."

"So I could have been your mistress longer?" And this was our turning point.

Akira swung his legs over the edge of the bed, turning his back to me. "I won't insult you, Ginger, by asking you to be my mistress."

"Then what will you ask?"

"I can ask nothing of you. You've given me everything already."

"Would you leave your wife for me?"

"I don't know."

"Do you love her at all?"

"Not in the way I love you."

"You don't love me, you're infatuated with me."

It seemed we had reached a characteristic impasse in male-female relations: *he* is content with the status quo; *she* wants to know where this goes from here. I even started to think about whether Akira and Megumi could get an annulment, were they to divorce. Annulments are given if the couple has some impediment to the validity of their marriage, so I started to wonder if Akira and Megumi are married in the eyes of the Church. Now, as I write it, this line of reasoning strikes me as dubious, but I couldn't keep myself from thinking about it. I wish there were some way I could have both my religion and this man.

"Were you involved with the principal's wife?"

"Don't be ridiculous."

"Why ridiculous? She's attractive."

"For God's sake, Ginger, she's the principal's wife. Who on a faculty sleeps with the principal's wife?"

I almost laughed, thinking of Jim-Bob.

"Then what did she say to you at intermission?"

He sounded exasperated. "She said you are a beautiful woman."

"What did she mean by that?"

"How can I know that? Maybe that you are a beautiful woman. Look, Ginger, we need to talk."

"What do you want to say?"

"What has kept you from men for so long?"

This hardly seemed any of Akira's business. I got up from the pink bed and went into the bathroom. I had left the fan on to give my clothes a chance to dry; the switch was still on, but the fan no longer worked. Under the harsh lighting, the mirrors all around drew attention to my reddened breasts and nipples and flushed cheeks. I took another shower, this time with hot, steamy water. I couldn't get enough of it. I soaked my hair with it, washed my body with it, I even opened my mouth and drank it. When I got out of the shower, the mirror was fogged up, and I looked down at my red hands, belly, and feet as I dried myself. I wanted visual proof that my body was still attached to my mind. Not only that, but I wanted to hear the voice, the voice in my head, the one that helps me figure out what to do when I'm in a jam. I've ignored it often enough. Where was that voice when I needed it? I couldn't hear it, and I couldn't see my way out.

I wiped off a circle in the middle of the mirror. As I dressed, my clothes at first felt odd, like they belonged to someone else. The blackish hair I saw in the mirror fooled me for a moment, making me think it was another woman in that love hotel, not me, but before long I saw who it was: me, Ginger O'Neill, American, Caucasian, entering middle age, and, as I touched my cross with my eyes, religious. I know it's banal to look in the mirror and realize something, but that's what happened. Maybe that's why some metaphors become clichés—they are real, they contain truth.

As I looked at myself, Joyce's Stephen Dedalus crossed my consciousness. There he sat, in the chapel of his Jesuit school during a retreat, a priest enumerating for him and his schoolmates all the many ways they would burn in hell, as well as spelling out for them the various ways in which their senses would be affected by their damnation. I knew, as I looked at my partially obscured self in the mirror, that I had two things to do. One was to get out of the relationship with Akira. The other was to face the truth about Steve.

When I came out of the bathroom, Akira was in his robe. He had opened the draperies and was looking out the window. "I'm sorry," he said.

"Don't be. I expected too much."

"No."

"Go back to your wife."

"My wife and I have no relationship. We lead separate lives."

His comments made me feel both hopeful and hopeless—hopeful that Akira could be mine and hopeless that I could walk away from him easily. I picked up my purse.

"Just tell me one thing, Ginger, will you?"

I nodded.

"Tell me, why me? Why did you wait all these years to get involved with a man, and then it was me? You could have any man. What am I to you?"

Again it crossed my mind that he, and others, might think I got involved with Akira to win the partnership. That was even more horrifying than the truth—that I was not in control of my desires. I had put so much at risk getting involved with him, my morals, my self-respect, his marriage, the partnership. To think people might think I'm a shallow opportunist. I'd rather they think I am in love with Akira than either shallow or an opportunist!

"Because you are as different from my husband as any man I have ever met." The statement was the first step toward the truth, a truth I knew I had to face, and I might as well start by facing it with Akira, the man it mattered to most.

"Why? Why was that important to you?"

I was appreciating that I meant more to him than a summertime, under-the-boardwalk romance; a quick liaison. Akira was genuinely concerned about me, or at least about the dynamics of our relationship.

"Why, Ginger? What did your husband do to you?"

"Nothing. He did nothing." Although he did.

"Then what? Was your love, *is* your love for him so strong that you can't bear to be reminded of your loss?"

I had to let it go. "The tunnel collapse that buried my husband? He wasn't alone when he died. My husband died in the arms of another woman."

I had never let myself visualize Steve's death before, not the way it actually happened. I had never uttered those words before, not even silently to myself, not in my most private, soul-searching moments. Or maybe I hadn't searched my soul since Steve's death; I had just pretended to. I had trained my mind. Every time it started to wander toward the truth, I changed its direction, I changed its course.

Akira led me over to the chair. He dressed quickly and sat on the edge of the bed. He fidgeted with his cigarettes but didn't light one.

"Tell me. Tell me what happened."

"Shortly after Steve's death, I went into his office to sign some papers and collect his personal effects. I saw a woman there. She was in the hall, holding a conversation with a colleague, and I recognized her from the services for Steve. She hadn't impressed me as particularly polished at the funeral home, unlike most of the others from Steve's office who came to pay their respects. I had put it down to her personality; I figured she wasn't the type who made a good public appearance. When she and the man she was talking to said hello to me in that hallway, I saw how stunning she was. Tall and muscular, with an intensity in her expression that you don't often see. Her voice was husky. Seductive."

"Don't tell me she had been a man."

"Not that I know of," I said. "But there *was* something strange about her. She had a locket hanging from a chain around her neck, and the locket—well, Steve's mother had one just like it. It was among her things when she died. It held Steve's high school graduation picture."

Akira closed his eyes. I went on.

"I didn't say anything then to the woman, but when I got home I looked through all Steve's things and couldn't find the locket."

"Your husband had given it to the woman."

"It took me some weeks to work up my courage, but eventually I went back to Steve's office. I waited outside the building's lobby until the woman came down the elevator and headed for the parking deck. She was wearing the locket. I stopped her and told her it was just like one my husband had, one that I couldn't find. I couldn't believe how bold I was. I had never done anything like that, confront someone like that."

"What did she say?"

"I'd caught her totally off guard. She broke down, cried and cried, with grief, with guilt, I don't know. She admitted she and Steve had been carrying on a relationship for several years. When I said I didn't believe her, that my husband came home to me every night, she reminded me that he had kept late hours at the office. And that he'd often taken business trips. She was right, of course. She opened the locket, and there was Steve's picture, which I could barely see, my eyes and my brain were having so much trouble focusing."

"Ginger—"

"She also said she was glad Steve wasn't alone at the end. She was with him when he died. When I heard that, I turned from her and ran down the street, ran for blocks and blocks. When I couldn't go any farther, I found myself by the river, and I was soaked with sweat. It was hours later, way past dark, before I could move."

"So you never wanted to be in a relationship with a man who reminds you of your husband. You don't want to be hurt again."

"You are entirely different from Steve. Except for one thing."

"I think I know what that is."

"You've betrayed your wife the way Steve betrayed me."

"My wife knows I'm not in love with her."

"I thought my husband loved me."

"He probably did. People aren't perfect, Ginger."

"I know."

"Did you think you were perfect?"

"Of course not. I just didn't think I was so evil," I told him. I looked at my ring. "Listen, I identify with your wife, regardless whether she thinks you love her, and regardless whether she loves you. You are her husband. What's at stake between you and me isn't only private. It's public too."

"Meaning?"

"There are things just as or more important than what one or two people want. There's the community, the people around them. The family."

Akira got up from the bed and retraced his steps to the window. "Your husband hurt your pride. Can you forgive him?"

"I don't know. He hasn't asked for my forgiveness. What I do know is I can't see you again."

"I was afraid you'd say that."

"I'm sorry, Akira."

"I want to be a part of your life. I don't know in what way, but I want to be part of your future. Don't regret this day, Ginger, and don't regret me."

He turned back to the window, and there was something about the moment—I wanted it never to end. I sat and stared at his reflection in the glass, I don't know for how long.

"I must go," I finally said. "I have packing to do."

"I'll see you home."

"I'll find my way home."

"Ginger, it's difficult, the route home. How will you manage?"

"I'll manage."

As the door shut automatically behind me, I thought of our conversation at lunch about one bite of blowfish ending a life, and I thought of Akira as one man who has irrevocably ended a part of mine. Before Steve's death, before I knew that he'd betrayed me, I had welcomed sensuality, for I had little or nothing to fear from it. In the past twelve years, though, I'd given it up, for I had been wounded by sensuality, albeit not my own. I turned my back on my erotic self. Could I continue to deny that side of myself? How would I do that? And why should I? I've been stuck, unable to move forward, because I've been angry with my dead husband, and because I haven't been honest about what I need.

Out on the street, each intersection greeted me as if it were one of life's decisions, the first decision small, the next one large; one important, the next trivial; again and again and so on, each simply an intersection, but each decision nevertheless significant, individually as well as collectively.

I was absorbed by the meaning of the decisions I'd made and soon found myself within a tangle of constricted streets. I passed what was probably an entrance to the subway but didn't feel like trying to negotiate the mass transit system. I didn't see police stations or anyone in the street to ask for help. Still, I went on.

Because I know Japan is generally safe, even for women, even at night, I wasn't panicking, but the shops would soon be closing and most people would be going home for the night. Around the last corner I came upon an open doorway, loud Caribbean music blaring from the sound system beyond it. The doorway led to a bar, and I went in. There was a bartender behind the counter and a few lone drinkers slouched on stools. I saw some booths in the murky light, but no people in them.

I shoulder bowed to the bartender. He dipped his head.

"Taxi?"

"Eh?"

"Taxi," I repeated, more slowly.

"Ah, *takushi*," he said.

"Hai. Takushi."

The bartender turned down the music and called to the back of the room. For a moment there was no response, but then I heard the shuffling of soles as an old man in dirty clothes moved hesitantly towards us from a darkened booth. The bartender spoke to him again. The old man nodded.

"Takushi," said the bartender to me again, and inclined his head toward the old man, following up with something incomprehensible.

The old man headed for the door, and I followed him. In the next block down the street he fumbled to unlock a dark sedan. The car didn't look like a taxi. He opened one of the back doors. For an instant I was unresolved, in the next I bent over and crawled in.

I found my piece of paper with the Murakamis' address and handed it to the old man. I had written out the words, in romaji, before I'd even left Nether Gorge. The man examined it under the dome light of the car, turned it over, saw that the back was blank, and muttered. He climbed out of the car and headed toward the bar. I took this as a good sign. I decided he wasn't a murderer.

The old man returned five minutes later, and I smelled liquor on him. He started the car and drove us out of the neighborhood, then into another, and another, and still another. In the pale yellow street lamplights, rhythmically spaced, I made out the driver's hunched shoulders, his grimy windshield, the cracked plastic seats with their stuffing falling out. The misery of this man's life. The misery of *my* life. My lonely, yearning life.

Akira had asked me if I could let it go, if I could forgive Steve. I never heard Steve ask for my forgiveness, but sometimes I'm deaf, sometimes I don't pay attention, sometimes I don't want to hear. Even if Steve, wherever he is, never did beg my pardon, I had it in my power to forgive him. There *is* such a thing as unilateral forgiveness. I didn't need anyone's permission to take this step. In fact, I had loved Steve so much that if he had asked me for a divorce, I probably would have agreed to it; I wanted him to be happy. If my love was that great, then I should love both him and myself enough to take the next step—forgiving him, and setting myself free.

It was time to quit holding it inside, but letting go of my pain overwhelmed me, there in that dingy, old taxi. My sobs came quietly at first, and then in heaves. The more embarrassed my crying made me, the more I cried. Tears that had been in me for years made their way out, tears that I'd bottled up at each opportunity. They were tears of abandonment, tears of shame, tears of guilt; they were tears for all the omissions and commissions and impulsive decisions of my life, tears for things I have done and for things that have been done to me. They were tears for the lost years, the lost possibilities, of my life. I cried enough to atone for the sins of people I don't know, have never seen, have never heard of, for the sins of people who have been dead for millennia, for the sins of people yet to be conceived. I shed tears for our lot in life, for original sin.

As the cab turned into the Murakamis' neighborhood, I dried my face on Sakiko's terrycloth towel. Like the old man, sliding the steering wheel through the circles his gloved hands were making, I was turning a corner of my own. And I could see around that bend no better than he could see through the filmy windows of his car.

Maybe some day Akira will be available, and I'll have to ask myself if I would want to marry a divorced man. Meanwhile, I won't be the person to split up his marriage. I'll always be grateful to Akira—grateful for his friendship, his compassion, the way he seemed to understand me. Perhaps I'll be the spur he needs to move ahead; his life has been just as frozen as mine. Perhaps that's even what drew us together—our inertia. Not choosing *is* choosing, not moving *is* moving—backwards.

I will never forget this day. I'll never forget Akira and being set free. And I'll never forget Japan, the rainy season I lived through in the summer of 2000, and the Osaka heat.

Monday, July 24, 2000
Dear Bernie,

By the time you read this, I should already be home. Do you remember the question I always ask after our trips— what did you learn on your travels? I'd like to tell you what I've learned so far, but this time my answer is more abstract than that I learned how to use the Paris Métro system, that I learned how to order a meal in Berlin, or that I learned that the English enjoy a wicked sense of humor.

Bernie, on this trip I have learned about myself. I've learned my feelings run deeper than my mind can fathom. I've learned that to some extent my head can't control my body. It can't control some sensations my body has—muggy air bringing moisture to the small of my back, dehydration causing me to faint, a man's glance attracting me. I've learned I have to deal with these feelings, good or bad, and that I can't continue to deny that I have them.

I've also learned that I don't always make the best choices. I could say it's unfortunate that we can't take back our poor choices, yet I don't think it's unfortunate. Who wants to spend her entire life with a finger on the rewind button? We make our choices and take the consequences. That's the only way we make progress.

Bernie, I know you've made some bad choices this summer. I just wanted you to know that I have too. Let's move on together, not regretting what we've done so much as learning from our experiences. I am no better or worse a person than you are or Aunt Reggie is or than your father or grandparents were. We all work to control our impulses. Sometimes we do that well, sometimes not so well. Let's go forward, helping each other, and looking across our entire lives, not focusing on moments of wrongdoing but on the overall pattern we've created, the overall picture we paint of ourselves. I hope you'll help me do this for myself. You can rely on me to be there for you.

I have more to tell you, but the Murakamis are calling me. We must leave for the airport now. I just wanted you to know I'll never forsake my responsibility to nurture and instruct you. Then, when you are my age, and I'm old, I can rely on you to comfort me with the goodness of the woman you've become. Praise God for mothers and daughters, Bernie, for they are the means by which the world's wisdom is passed along.

With all my love,
Mom

FOURTEEN

Sushi

Osaka and the mainland shrink in the minivan's wake as Hiro aims at Kansai Airport, in Osaka Bay. Mr. and Mrs. Murakami and their guest pass a towering hotel to starboard as they head onto the bridge that leads to the airport, out in the water. The airport dazzles the eyes, lying as it does in the blinding sea, a sea Ginger crossed earlier this month on her ferry ride from Awaji Island, a sea that washes around the lower extremities of the dragon.

"Airport is sinking, Ginger," Sakiko says. "Runway is undergoing big—what's the word?"

"Shoring up," says Hiro.

Ginger will miss Japan—the planes with Pokémon characters painted on their tails; hot baths; beer in vending machines; even the tunnels and bridges. She'll miss the way her senses were sparked here, in ways they haven't been at home.

"Your time with us is almost up, Jinja!"

"Is there anything you wish you had done, Ginger?"

"I could have eaten some more sushi." Ginger is still wishing for horse mackerel. "And I would have liked a rickshaw ride."

Sakiko laughs. "You have one next time. Is Japan what you expected?"

"Yes, though for rainy season it hasn't rained much. Except for my first night, in Tokyo."

"Weather is not so bad while you are with us. Come back next year!"

"I just remembered—Hiro, do you know what happened to that print I made with Teru? I'd forgotten all about it. I liked that piece."

"I meant to mention to you, Tanabe-*sensei* asked if he could keep your painting."

"What does he want it for?"

"He wants to frame it for the conference room. Is that okay with you?"

"Ginger, you can see it next summer when you visit."

"Sounds good to me."

On her way out of the house, Ginger had checked her e-mail one last time. There was a note from Bernie:

Mom—

Aunt Reggie won't let me go anywhere.
I can't wait to see you! Have a good trip home.

B.

And there was a last note from Ginger's sister.

Ginger:

Bernie and I are doing fine. I think her recent experience has made her more mature.

Too bad you don't know when the committee meets next. It would be nice if you could fly home victorious.

See you soon.

Reggie

"I don't suppose any of the other teachers will be at the airport," Ginger says.

"What do you think?" Sakiko asks her husband.

"They would not be able to get away from their classes."

"How did you get away, Hiro?"

"I am your official host. It is expected that I take you to the airport. The principal sent a substitute for my classes."

In the terminal, Hiro pushes her luggage ahead as Ginger and Sakiko tail him. Short of the check-in counter, he is stopped by a slender woman. She's dressed in a sarong skirt and matching blouse of polished cotton. The ensemble is in muted shades of bottle green and gold. The skirt falls just above her knees. Initially, from a distance, the woman looks barefoot, but closer up it's evident she's wearing the sheerest of stockings and sling-back pumps, the pumps the same color as her legs. She has perfectly coiffed hair—ivory black, chin length, turned under slightly. Her makeup, especially her eye shadow, looks professionally applied. She puts her right hand out to Ginger.

Hiro clears his throat. "Jinja, I want to introduce Sato Megumi."

"I am pleased to meet you, Ginger-san."

Akira's wife. She's lovely. Ginger takes her hand. "Megumi-san. *Hajime mashite.*"

Megumi extends her left hand to Ginger with a small bouquet that catches the light in an unusual way. "You enjoy sushi?"

"I do." Ginger accepts the offering. *"Arigato gozaimasu."*

Megumi nods. So this is the woman against whom Ginger has sinned. She deserves more recognition than an acknowledgement of a favor, but the tongue that Ginger had in the mouth of Megumi's husband yesterday is suddenly incapable of functioning. This teacher of language can't quite figure out what to say.

"I want to beg your pardon," Ginger utters at last. But what does Ginger mean, begging Megumi's pardon? Is she apologizing to her? If she were to apologize, it would be to clear her own tab, not to make Megumi comfortable. "Thank you for all your help when I was away from home, Megumi-san. I mean, when I was on Awaji."

Megumi nods again. Ginger could be honest and add, *When your husband and I were on Awaji,* but she won't muster the truth this time. Indeed, better that she not, that she exercise some restraint, come charity.

"You were in a bad spot, Ginger-san. Your daughter needing you." Now *here* is a woman who does the right thing.

"Yes, thank you."

"Jinja, we need to get your trunk checked."

The practicalities of the journey had slipped Ginger's mind. "Just let me be sure I locked it." She bends down to test the padlock, and when she straightens up, Megumi is gone.

As Ginger waits in the check-in line, she studies the bouquet and discovers it's not a bunch of flowers at all. Colorless, slender plastic straws culminate in sheaths of transparent cellophane, each of the coverings closed by a short piece of pipe cleaner in a bright color—red, pink, lemon yellow, blue. Inside each sheath, stuck fast to its lollipop stick, is a lozenge of hard-candy sushi. Ginger recognizes the striated salmon, the *futomaki*, the *maguro*, the ikura. What she doesn't recognize is the yellow rhombus striped with *nori*. She turns to Sakiko.

"*Kazunoko*. Herring roe. Expensive. *Yellow diamonds*, we call it. For special occasions, like New Year."

Why did Megumi come to meet Ginger? And what does her gift of sucker sushi mean? Is she saying, "You can have my husband sexually, but I will have him otherwise?" Or is she staking her exclusive claim to him? Was she above all curious about Ginger, the way Ginger was about Megumi? Is she, like her husband, considering abandoning their marriage? In any case, being part of a threesome is a disagreeable place to be. The flesh and blood of Megumi has added to Ginger's proof that this is no graceful matter, this matter of Akira. Seeing Megumi strengthens Ginger's resolve that she won't come between them, no matter how drawn to Megumi's husband Ginger is. She will leave Akira to wage his marriage battle himself, and when she gets home she'll keep company with men who are properly available. She will allow herself to become romantically involved. She may even date divorced men; religious issues will work themselves out. Ginger is at last free of the pain of her husband's betrayal. She can love again.

Sakiko hands Ginger last-minute gifts: a folding fan for Bernie, a set of chopsticks for Reggie, a lacy pink handkerchief for Ginger. She hugs Ginger, and both women cry. Sakiko reaches down for Ginger's hands and holds her at arm's length.

"I want to remember exactly how you look, Ginger."

"Thank you for all you've done, Sakiko. You've been perfect hosts."

"Our pleasure."

Ginger turns to Hiro. He takes her hand and claps her on the back.

"Thank you for everything, Hiro."

"You're welcome. Or should I say *No problem*?"

"The kids back home say that."

Hiro pulls Ginger to the side. "You know, Jinja, I've been meaning to mention, my name is pronounced with the tip of your tongue up against the back of your top teeth. Like this." He says *ro* so it sounds more like *lo*. "Next time you come, you can practice."

"May I look in your mouth?" Ginger is trying to keep her composure, distracting herself from the feelings she's having, emotions that are about to flood her.

"If you like."

Hiro opens his mouth and tightens his cheek muscles, insinuating his tongue somewhere behind his front top teeth.

"I've been pronouncing it wrong all along. I know it's corny, but I'll always think of you as *Hero*."

"Okay."

"I want to thank you again, especially for taking care of me the day I got sick."

"Did you enjoy your trip?"

"Yes, but I wish I could start it over."

"Don't do that!" He looks blank for a moment. "Jinja, I'm afraid I forgot to tell you the most important thing. The committee met first thing this morning."

"Oh?" It takes courage for Ginger to continue to listen. It would be easier for her if she walked through security now. "And did they decide anything?"

"Does your school want us as a partner school?"

"I thought the committee knew that."

"They liked the cooking show. You gave our school good publicity. But your comments to the committee last week were the deciding factor."

"Oh."

"People can't stop talking about that meeting. Your honesty made a lasting impression. This morning's vote was unanimous. If Confederate wants us, we want Confederate."

So Ginger has gotten what she came to Japan for.

"Do you know, Hiro, was Akira at the meeting?"

"He was not. Take care of yourself, Jinja."

"You, too."

Our traveler passes through security and begins her walk toward the gate. She is already wondering what food she'll be served on the plane. Having taken no more than a few steps toward the gate, the pressure of a tap on her shoulder causes her to turn and find an elderly woman speaking to her and pointing backwards. Ginger looks back toward security. She sees one person there, his face all but pressed to the glass wall, his right hand, palm toward Ginger, waving back and forth the way members of the British royal family do. Akira is wearing his geranium shirt. Ginger bows to him, and he bows in return. Raising her right hand, she drops a kiss onto the fleshy side of her fingers and blows the kiss to Akira. He catches it and touches his heart with his hand. She stands and looks at him, until she's the only passenger left in the boarding area. Then, juggling her carry-on bags and turning toward the skywalk, she wrests from the sticky tape of Megumi's bouquet the ikura sushi lollipop. It's bad Japanese manners to eat and walk at the same time, but Ginger is beyond worrying about that. She peels the cellophane from the sucker, lifts the candy to her mouth, and takes a good, long, puckering pull. The thought that Megumi might have poisoned the candy crosses Ginger's mind as an absurdity one would read about in a book. She casts it aside as a childish and extravagant notion.

The boarding agent rips Ginger's ticket in two, handing her half. "Thank you for flying with us, Mrs. O'Neill. We hope to see you again soon."

Monday, July 24

I boarded and found my seat, this time on the aisle. A woman with headphones is at the window. She hasn't looked at me. I'm planning to keep my diary in my lap, even through take-off. I haven't taken any drugs. I want to see if I'm truly afraid of flying, or if I've just been afraid of the risks that forward motion entails.

It really threw me to meet Megumi.

At the gate I tore a fresh sheet out of this journal and scribbled a note on it. I was going to hold it up for Akira to read through the glass, but I had second thoughts; something was telling me not to show it to him. My note—I'll keep it here in my diary as evidence of an impulse that I did *not* act on—reads, "Let me know if anything changes…"

Akira knows where to find me.

The flight attendants have prepared for take-off. I need a manicure. I hope Bernie will paint my nails with Fiji Lilac again, if that's still her favorite color. And here is this narrow gold band on my left hand, the ring I've never removed since Steve put it on my finger on our wedding day.

We're queueing up for take-off.

As we were waiting there in line a few minutes ago, I unfastened the gold chain from the front of my neck, where the clasp had worked itself, and removed the chain with the cross Steve gave me as an engagement present. I would have preferred a diamond ring, but Steve thought I'd like the cross better. I pulled the plain band from my finger. The ring slid down the chain and fit neatly around the cross. For a moment, I held them in the palm of my hand, then I reclasped the chain at the back of my neck. I can feel it there now. When I get home I'll put all of it in my jewelry box. Bernie has always admired the cross. It will be hers some day.

Our wheels are up.

The woman next to me is snoring. I'm feeling as though I could take a nap myself, but I want to finish this journal entry. I'm stating for the record: it was not my religion that inhibited me from romance. I was afraid to love again, afraid to get hurt again. But now I see that I can love again, and get hurt again, for leaving Akira is the most painful thing I've done since—well, I can't remember when I've taken such a painful step.

No, the business about divorce was a ruse to keep men away and to keep people from pestering me about dating. I'd used the dodge so often I'd come to believe it myself. Funny how the mind works.

My faith is a stickler about divorce. Marriages are serious business, and every effort should be taken to keep them intact. But when they're beyond repair, there ought to be a way for people to move on without sacrificing love for the rest of their lives. The annulment process allows Catholics to live within the technicalities of the law, but if an annulment is nothing other than a religious divorce, it should be acknowledged as such. Either the Church accepts divorce or it doesn't. The faithful can see the slippery-sloped game that's being played with annulments. It makes an august institution look less than august.

I could give up my religion, but, as I've written in these pages, I love the Catholic Church. I'd rather stay and try to work within its limitations. The Church is made up of people, people who are no less sinful than the rest of the world, even if sometimes we like to think otherwise. People must learn right from wrong, their consciences must be formed, and a faith performs that function. On the other hand, *is* there really an objective truth? I'm not sure that right and wrong are black and white. One person's reality is another's fantasy. Our spiritual lives, our situations, are so intricate, so idiosyncratic, that black and white resolution seems impossible.

I don't know what to think about divorce, but I won't be limiting my dating options. The important thing is that, finally, I'm willing to move ahead. I'll go moment by moment and see what happens.

In that lively discussion Akira and I had after dinner in his room at the ryokan, he said to me, "Ginger, you know you're not a character in a novel, don't you?" I was amused at his question, but it rings true. Maybe I do think of myself as a character in a novel, especially given all that's happened to me on this trip. Without a doubt, I've been energized by keeping this journal. I don't know that I have anything new to say; there are new *ways* to say things, however. And literature can give meaning to life.

One day I may type up this record of July 2000, changing the names and faces to protect the guilty. I could try to publish it as fiction. Someone, somewhere, might want to read it. I know it would be hard to believe that all these things happened to one person in three short weeks, but, except for the odd detail here or there, I swear every word of it is true.

ACKNOWLEDGEMENTS

I owe debts of gratitude for help with *Osaka Heat*—

to Kathie, Dee, Kathy, Robin, Martha, Sue, Neal, Val, Leone, Jennifer S., Joyce, Paulena, Fujimi, Harumi, Misako, Lorie, Christa and Jennifer K., and to Nani and my classmates at the Writer's Center,

to my husband, Herb, and our sons, Ed and George,

and to Taka and Maureen.

ABOUT THE AUTHOR

Osaka Heat is Mary Claire Mahaney's first novel. She has written short stories, poetry, essays, and reviews of the arts. A retired lawyer, Mahaney lives with her family in Virginia, where she is at work on a children's book. For more information, visit her website at www.maryclairemahaney.com.

Printed in the United States
82181LV00001B/12